The Design of Computer-Based Instruction

The Design of Computer-Based Instruction

Eleanor L. Criswell

Science Applications International Corporation
McLean, Virginia

Macmillan Publishing Company
NEW YORK

Collier Macmillan Publishers
LONDON

Macmillan Publishing Company
866 Third Avenue, New York, New York 10022

Collier Macmillan Canada, Inc.

LIBRARY OF CONGRESS CATALOGING-IN-PUBLICATION DATA

Criswell, Eleanor L.
The design of computer-based instruction.
Bibliography: p.
Includes index.
1. Computer-assisted instruction — Authoring
programs. I. Title.
LB1028.66.C75 1989   371.3'9445   87-35034
ISBN 0-02-325603-6

Printing: 1 2 3 4 5 6 7   Year: 9 0 1 2 3 4 5

Preface

This book approaches the design and evaluation of computer-based instruction (CBI) from psychological and practical perspectives. It emphasizes knowledge from psychology and educational research that is fundamental to CBI design and evaluation. It also describes a systematic design and evaluation process that produces successful courseware if this knowledge is used. These themes are in contrast to writings on CBI which discuss types and examples of CBI, technological advances in the computer industry, and computer code. The book provides the rationale for CBI design and is a "how to" for designers and users, not a CBI description.

This book is based on research from three specialty areas: learning psychology, cognitive science, and human factors. Learning psychology and the functional analysis of behavior offer the principles and processes by which students interact with new material and come to learn. Cognitive science deals with the structure of effective instructional material. Human factors psychology, the study of how people interact with inanimate objects, offers information about student–computer interfaces and advises how to lay out material on a computer screen to maximize student use of the material in an efficient manner. This book emphasizes findings from all these fields.

At the same time, the text is not a literature review. Much of the book consists of practical applications and examples. These examples illustrate the points and serve as a resource for CBI designers. The examples of CBI design and evaluation are based on research on CBI, research on instruction in other media besides the computer, and on professional experiences of CBI designers, including the author.

This book is for student and practicing CBI designers; most CBI designers work in the areas of education, psychology, and computer science. The book is also for the many CBI designers who have found themselves, relatively unprepared, thrust into the field of CBI design by the computer revolution. As the field grows, consumers of CBI will quickly become more discriminating, and soon the marketplace will accept only that CBI which not only really teaches, but also teaches efficiently and pleasurably. This book teaches how to design effective, efficient, pleasurable CBI in any context, based on sound principles.

CBI designers work in diverse fields, from elementary school teachers who produce their own drill and practice programs to those who design innovative CBI for highly technical subject matter. In this book we discuss the teaching function of courseware — determining purposes and content, sequencing topics, increasing productive student interaction — and the evaluation function of courseware designers, writers, and teachers. Examples in the book portray a wide range in subject matter. The reader will be able to use the examples as a resource, given an understanding of the basic concepts. The use of jargon and invented terms has been avoided except in cases where the term has been well defined. This will make easier more general use of the material.

More people purchase and use CBI than design and develop it. CBI users must know about CBI design and evaluation so they will be able to select good courseware for their use. As more high-quality courseware becomes available, teachers will find that purchased software meets their needs, but they must know how to evaluate quality in the courseware marketplace. This book teaches how to evaluate quality: from a fine-grained analysis of any single practice interaction to an evaluation of the cost and training effectiveness of a CBI module.

The topic sequence of the book is design first, then evaluation. In Chapter 1 we introduce the history and types of CBI. Chapter 2 provides an integrated model of the processes involved in effective CBI design. In Chapters 3 through 7 we discuss CBI design in detail. Chapter 3 presents a 10-step process used to design, produce, and evaluate CBI. Special attention is devoted in Chapter 3 to context analysis, knowledge engineering, stating instructional objectives, communicating with the computer programmer, and programming languages. In Chapter 4 we describe the student–computer interface, especially the frame. This chapter was placed early so that readers would understand important aspects of frame display in the examples in subsequent chapters. In Chapters 5, 6, and 7 we describe sequencing and writing the important elements in CBI. In Chapter 5 we discuss ways to sequence topics. In Chapter 6 we discuss how to construct and intersperse introductions, interactions, remedial branches, reviews, and tests. In Chapter 7 we discuss how to tailor interactions for four student performance levels: acquisition, fluency building, generalization, and proficiency maintenance. Courseware evaluation and revision is discussed in Chapter 8. Four types of evaluation are described: structural, functional, user opinion, and cost-effectiveness.

Study questions are provided at the end of every chapter. The questions cover the important points in the chapter. Definition questions require a short answer that comes directly from the text. Discussion questions require a longer answer and some synthesis. Students can answer the questions orally or in writing, alone or in class; instructors should determine how best to use the questions. Periodic review of the questions will help the student maintain mastery of the material.

Many people have encouraged me, pointed me toward literature, inspired me, and critiqued my ideas as I have written this book. I am most indebted to my husband, psychologist Dr. Bruce Wetherby. Bruce reviewed every chapter, discussed issues with me, and stimulated me to consider perspectives I had not yet considered. I am also indebted to the editorial staff at Macmillan and their book reviewers, who have been supportive throughout. Two of my associates provided thoughtful reviews: Dr. Ward Cates of George Mason University in Fairfax, Virginia, and Dr. Robert Hays of the Naval Training Systems Center in Orlando, Florida. In addition, Dr. Dexter Fletcher of Institutes for Defense Analyses in Alexandria, Virginia provided a valuable critique of Chapter 2. Several others graciously provided samples from CBI lessons they had developed which I have used as illustrations throughout the book: Dr. Nadine Hackler, University of Florida, Gainesville; Ms. Bonnie Hobson, U.S. Senate Computer Center, Washington, D.C.; Dr. Joseph Psotka, U.S. Army Research Institute, Alexandria, Virginia; and Ms. Catherine M. Taggart, Merrill Lynch, Training Technology, Plainsboro, New Jersey. Finally, I am appreciative of the support of my colleagues at Science Applications International Corporation.

E. L. C.

Contents

List of Figures

CHAPTER 1

Introduction to Computer-Based Instruction

The main topics in this chapter are:

- *Definitions of terms in computer-based instruction (CBI)*
- *Optimizing the use of CBI*
- *History of CBI*
- *Scope of CBI applications*
- *Importance of hardware and software in CBI*

Definitions

The term *computer-based instruction* (CBI) refers to any use of a computer to present instructional material, provide for active participation of the student, and respond to student action. Very simply, the goal of CBI is to teach. The term "computer-based instruction" is used in this book; the terms "computer-assisted instruction" and "computer-aided learning" express the same concepts.

Learning is the relatively permanent change in the student's state of knowledge or skill. Learning is a process. Learning progresses from an initial level of poor knowledge and performance to levels of increased knowledge and much better performance, when and only when something or someone, such as a computer teacher, supports a student's progress.

Teaching consists of the teacher (human or computer) support activities that cause a student to learn. These activities include presenting new instructional challenges, providing enough practice, reviewing when necessary, informing the student about the correctness of his or her responses, allowing the student to discover for himself or herself when learning certain skills, and keeping track of the student's progress. The understanding that learning progresses as a function of teaching activities is fundamental to designing CBI.

Teaching in CBI is accomplished by the use of a computer (hardware), programs to make the computer operate (software), and a program designed especially to administer the instruction (courseware). This book focuses on the design and evaluation of courseware.

Hardware includes the physical, electronic, and electromechanical components of computers. CBI may be designed for use on a variety of computers, from large mainframes that support individual student stations, to small home or personal computers. Effective CBI can be designed for a computer of any size.

Two types of *software* are involved in CBI. *Delivery system software* interfaces the student with the computer, and *authoring system software* interfaces the coursewriter with the computer (Bunderson, 1981).

Courseware refers, in a narrow sense, to programs that administer instruction (Futrell & Geisert, 1984), and in a broad sense, to those programs in addition to all handbooks and performance aids, and so on, which are the course material (Bunderson, 1981).

CBI in and of itself seldom constitutes an entire course. Usually, CBI is an adjunct to human instruction and is integrated into a course with other means of instruction. For example, course material might be presented by lecture, textbook review, or film, and by practice in the skill, provided by the computer. In some cases, CBI simulations provide advanced practice that would not be available in a classroom. Adjunct CBI can be used to present material and provide practice, and ancillary textbook reading may be assigned.

Optimizing the Use of CBI

CBI has been found to compare favorably with traditional instruction. A review of 51 studies conducted with sixth- through twelfth-grade students found that students in CBI classes scored in the 63rd percentile on final examinations, and students in conventional classes scored in the 50th percentile (Kulik, Bangert, & Williams, 1983). The effects of CBI tend to be greater for low achievers than for high achievers, and greater at the secondary level than at the college level, but this finding was not statistically significant in the review. The same review also found that students developed positive attitudes toward their CBI courses. As for a particular subject, CBI has been found to be more effective than traditional methods in teaching elementary and high school mathematics, for example (Kulik et al., 1983). College-level CBI has been found more effective than traditional methods in teaching physics, anesthesiology, and Russian (Chambers & Sprecher, 1980).

When can CBI be used effectively?

* When the subject matter does not change significantly over time, because changes in the topic require reprogramming.
* When repeated presentations of the same course are needed, because computers are excellent at repeating courses over and over without a decrease in proficiency due to fatigue.
* When actual practice of the skill being learned is important, because students using CBI can practice skills that would otherwise not be possible.
* When human teachers thereby spared the teaching time may productively engage in other important instructional activities. CBI does not replace teachers, but it permits teachers to perform other activities.

Perhaps the greatest danger in using CBI occurs when it is not integrated properly into the total curriculum. CBI must be examined carefully by the teacher to determine exactly what the CBI teaches. For example, many CBI programs provide practice but do not present and teach the material. A student given a CBI practice program without being prepared for it may well flounder and despair. In other cases, some CBI is given to students as a time filler without regard to its place in the curriculum. Instructional games can be misused in this way—given to students unprepared to play them, or given to students in the hope that something (anything) useful will be taught, without analyzing the game to see if anything really valuable is being taught. Proper integration of CBI into the total curriculum is a key to its success.

History of CBI

The rapid development and spread of CBI has been encouraged by society's pressures to educate large numbers of people, our knowledge about the psychological principles of teaching and learning, and the availability of the computer. Large-scale demands for education are nothing new in the United States, but our solutions to the problem have frequently been unsatisfactory. As more and more students arrived, class size increased. The addition of more teachers, more classrooms (often in trailers where school construction was too slow or too costly), even staggered school sessions, accommodated students, but did little to improve teaching or learning. The demand for teachers and courses continued.

More recently, the public has become dismayed at declining achievement on the part of students of normal intelligence. An entire discipline of special education has developed whose focus is those students who could not possibly survive in a regular classroom. About 10 percent of all school-age students spend time in a special education classroom. One might argue that many more students, many of whom now underachieve in regular classes, could benefit from special or improved learning environments. Education should be looking for cost-effective and training-effective methods of instruction. CBI provides the potential to provide instruction tailored to meet an individual student's needs, and at the same time, be relatively low cost.

In the early to mid-1950s, psychologists began to incorporate psychological principles of learning, derived from laboratory experiments with people and animals, into a practical framework for teaching courses. The pioneer in this area was B. F. Skinner, who himself had conducted important laboratory research in animal learning. Skinner first suggested that effective teaching hinged on the mastery of small steps, each building on the preceding step, active participation on the part of the student, and active participation on the part of the instructor to present the information in carefully sequenced bits and to assess the student's performance. Skinner also suggested that what we say, write, or think, whether in a social or an academic setting, was learned in much the same manner as we learn nonverbal activity.

Skinner and others began to develop programmed instruction. Early programs could be delivered in textbooks, radically reformatted (cf. Holland & Skinner, 1961). These programmed textbooks did not use paragraphs, but were formatted in small bits of information. Each bit of information contained a sentence or two, was carefully sequenced to build on previous bits, and required the student to answer questions correctly, check his or her own answers, then move on to the next bit. Hundreds of small bits made up a course.

Skinner (1968) notes that Pressey in the early 1920s developed a mechanical testing device that administered multiple-choice items one at a time. If the student gave the right answer, the next item appeared; otherwise, the student repeatedly answered the same question until the correct answer was selected. Pressey observed that learning occurred, and that perhaps the testing machines could also be used for teaching. In the 1950s and 1960s, Skinner and others developed mechanical devices that would present instruction. The benefit of teaching machines over programmed textbooks was that they helped assure that the student would answer all the questions in the lessons and not skip over important material.

Many educators resisted the machines and their programs because they felt the machines might displace teachers or impart instruction in an undesirable, mechanistic fashion. Skinner answered critics by saying that the machines would improve teacher–student interactions because the teacher would be freed of routine instructional presentation, drill, and testing duties. The teacher would thus have more time to interact with students in the capacity of an advisor or friend. Many instructional programs were prepared and for a while, enjoyed popularity. In many instances, however, students were not experienced at being active during instruction, and many expressed displeasure with programmed courses. Many of the courses were horribly boring because of their strict adherence to a certain format. Each bit was presented in the same way. Textbooks that have been strictly programmed are not popular today. However, the principles behind programmed instruction live on and underlie the design of much current CBI.

In the meantime, another machine, television, was being applied in education. Education at that time was trying to solve the problem of mass education. As White (1983) points out, CBI and instructional television are both examples of electronic learning, phenomena of a postindustrial society. White suggests that television changed education, even society itself, in several critical ways. First, television provided a means for students to learn autonomously. Second, television made learning very entertaining— more entertaining than traditional education. Further, television was easily available. In retrospect, we also know that home television has taught values to many people. CBI appears to share these important characteristics.

Educational television is available today, but its popularity has been eclipsed by many factors, including CBI. Like movies and textbooks, educational television does not allow for active participation on the part of students and teachers, and thus does not possess the instructional power of CBI. CBI allows for individualized instruction not available through television.

In the late 1950s and early 1960s, the computer, which previously had been used to make rapid mathematical calculations, began to be used in teaching. At Dartmouth was developed the computer programming language called BASIC, which processed words as well as numbers, and was used in writing instructional programs there. During that time, programmed instruction (as well as noninteractive textbook-style instruction) was incorporated into CBI. The fire was then fueled by the need for mass education.

Several major universities, including Dartmouth, Florida State University, the University of Illinois, the University of California, and California State University, were prominent in early CBI projects. The PLATO project developed at the University of Illinois helped make CBI available at many schools around the nation. Presently, a large number of PLATO courses is available, even to home computer owners, via telephone link to one of the large PLATO mainframe computers. Now most, if not all, universities have computer centers that provide primary (complete courses) or adjunctive (drills, refreshers, etc.) CBI. Exposure to CBI is viewed by many as mandatory in colleges, high schools, and even at the primary or toddler level.

Mainframe computers, each supporting numerous terminals, provide access to CBI for many students. However, smaller personal or microcomputers, which stand alone without a mainframe, flourish. Recent figures indicate that there are about 600,000 small computers in use in elementary and secondary schools, one for every 66 students (Eberts & Brock, 1987), 11,000,000 microcomputers in the home (Helm, 1984), and tens of thousands more computers in business, industry, and government. About 1 million personal computers are sold every year.

Applications in CBI

Professionals in computer science and education have used the computer in many educational contexts. The CBI most common in the past, *frame-based*, where an instructional program is presented frame by frame in a relatively fixed sequence, save for simple remedial loops, is now joined by other more flexible ways to present instruction by computer. Intelligent CBI, training simulations, and instructional games represent the more flexible types of CBI and are not frame-based. The remainder of this chapter describes several of these CBI applications, including:

- Lessons or tutorials
- Reinforced drill and practice
- Intelligent CBI

- Training simulations (presented on a computer screen)
- Instructional games
- Training simulators (pieces of equipment built for training purposes)
- Expert systems
- Embedded training
- Adaptive testing
- Computer-managed instruction

Common Basis for All Applications

CBI applications are developed from a common basis. As discussed in Chapter 2, functional or behavioral and structural or cognitive orientations suggest effective instructional designs. Skinner (1984) suggests four components of successful instruction (in any application) in the functional or behavioral tradition:

- Clear instructional objectives.
- Teaching substeps as a way to attain mastery of larger units.
- Allowing students to progress at their own rate.
- Carefully programmed (or sequenced) instruction.

As applied to the design of CBI applications, it is important that the instructional objectives be stated explicitly. It is good design to tell the student in advance what he or she will learn.

Determining the substeps required for teaching an instructional objective is a process called *concept analysis* or *task analysis*. The product of such an analysis is a set of prerequisite skills, steps that must be learned before the final goal is reached. Also required is a determination of the sequence in which the prerequisites or subskills should be taught.

The third component in Skinner's (1984) model, self-pacing, may be a way to use time more efficiently. As Skinner (1984) notes, without self-pacing, faster students are held behind, and slower students fall further and further behind. Current self-pacing procedures, however, have generated mixed results. It may be that current self-pacing procedures need to be revised to increase their effectiveness.

Finally, programmed instruction gets the learner to respond to the material. New material builds on previously learned material (Skinner, 1968). The sequencing of substeps is thus important in programming. In addition, programming of instructional events used to teach a substep is important. Becker, Englemann, and Thomas (1975) present 10 steps that may be used in programming

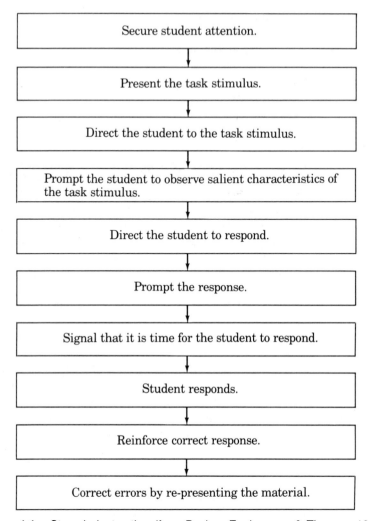

Figure 1.1. Steps in instruction (from Becker, Englemann, & Thomas, 1975).

the teaching of a small bit of instruction or task. Less sophisticated learners often require use of all 10 steps; as students advance, less importance may be placed on directions and prompts. These steps are presented in Figure 1.1.

Gagne (1977), a leading figure in the field of instructional design, has described several internal events derived from a structural or information-processing approach which may also be important to consider when developing instructional techniques. These internal cognitive processes are assumed to underlie the external events of instruction. Gagne describes the instructional process as beginning by securing a student's attention or motivation. This can be done by stating the lesson objective. Next, the student's selective perception is involved as the instructor directs the student's attention to the material. Review of previously learned material requires encoding and storage. New material is then put into memory. Daily review requires the student to retrieve information from memory. The student may be asked to transfer information and use it in a new way.

Tutorials

A CBI tutorial is simply a computer-presented lesson. There are two types of tutorials: linear and branching. A *linear program* presents every frame to every student. The presentation is much like a textbook, often heavily word oriented. Linear programs may be paced by the student and may include interesting graphics. The amount of instruction presented is the same for every student, but the time taken to complete a program varies from student to student. Variable times are due to self-pacing and review presented as a result of errors.

Unlike a textbook, a linear program presents information in carefully sequenced small bits, and the student is queried about each bit. The student cannot alter the forward progression of the program, except to pace it. The student may review information, but review may not be required by the program. Review in linear programs is usually a re-presentation of the material that has not been mastered.

Linear programs, first devised in the late 1950s and early 1960s, represented an educational revolution because they fostered individualized instruction. Today, these programs are still widely used, but other programming techniques, also for individualized instruction and more sensitive to students and their progress, are available.

Branching programs permit interaction with only those parts of the program that the student has not mastered. This is an improvement over linear programs. Branching programs include pretests of major sections in the program. The program computes the student score and advises the student to either skip over or complete the section.

In addition, branching programs often include review sequences that the student can select as needed. Students often indicate their desire for review by pressing a "help" key or typing in the word "help." These review sequences provide extra instruction not presented on the first pass through the program. Availability of several review sequences is quite helpful to students and decreases the likelihood that the student will give up and call for assistance from a teacher.

The type of feedback given to students in branching programs ranges from simple (such as "correct") to more elaborate (such as "You forgot to carry the 1. Please try again."). The quality of the feedback usually depends on the skill of the designer and the degree to which the programming language or system makes easy the provision of complex feedback.

In a branching tutorial, the amount of instruction presented depends on the student's performance. Branching tutorials may thus be said to be adaptive. Branching tutorials allow students to skip over material as soon as mastery is reached. Completion times thus vary from student to student.

Once branching CBI is designed, it is programmed using a general programming language such as BASIC or Pascal, a CBI authoring language such as TenCore or PILOT, or any of dozens of software programs specially designed for courseware creation (*authoring tools*) which are presently available, such as CSF Trainer 4000, QUEST or Scholar/Teach. The courseware programs developed using these methods contain the course content, instructional plan, and student record, all in a single program.

Reinforced Drill and Practice

A very common and important use of CBI is for reinforced drill and practice. The importance of reinforced drill and practice is to strengthen an acquisition or beginning-level performance until mastery is reached. Repetitive practice is important in learning some new skills. Drill and practice programs do not systematically introduce new material as tutorials do. Reinforced drill and practice programs are thus adjunct to tutorials.

Once learning progress begins and responding is stable, the prompts, cues, and feedback or reinforcers so important in introducing instruction may be used less and less often. A good reinforced drill and practice program will gradually fade out the prompts and reduce the number of responses that receive feedback.

Once mastery is reached, reinforced drill and practice is of little value except as periodic review. Reinforced drill and practice of a mastery level skill may also be used as a reinforcer, reward, or student-selected activity, particularly if the drill or practice is fun.

Drill and practice programs have proliferated, but their quality and use have dismayed many. First, many drill and practice programs are boring and unimaginative. Second, one value of these programs, to free instructors of mundane tasks and allow them

Selected category
is highlighted

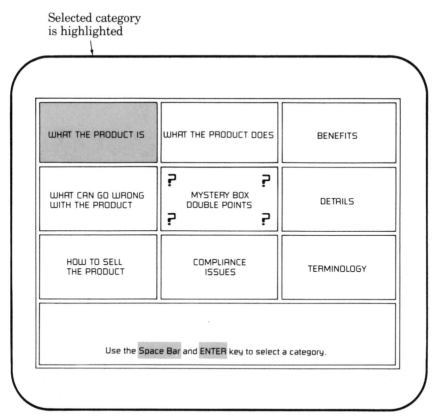

Figure 1.2. Reinforced drill and practice format (courtesy of Catherine M. Taggart, Merrill Lynch Training Technologies).

time to relate personally with students, has not yet been realized. This may be due to the fact that teachers are trained to administer drill and practice, not to attend to the needs of individuals (Helm, 1984.) Thus many teachers have not yet taken advantage of whatever good drill and practice programs may realize. Obviously, this need not remain true, but teacher training must consider this new situation in education.

Figure 1.2 presents an imaginative format for drill, developed by the Merrill Lynch Training Division. Nine categories of drill questions were developed. The student selects the drill category he or she wants (by pressing the keyboard space bar to move the highlight from category to category, stopping on the desired category). When the drill category is mastered, the Merrill Lynch corporate bull logo is placed in the box.

Intelligent CBI

Definition. Intelligent CBI (ICBI) is a recent advance in the field of CBI. Simply, ICBI involves the use of artificial intelligence programming for the purpose of making the CBI more responsive than traditional CBI. The notion is that for many subjects, a student will learn better with a personalized tutor that *understands* how the student is progressing and why the student is making errors.

Artificial intelligence programs are written with words, whereas conventional programs are written in lower level symbols (e.g., variables). Thus artificial intelligence programming allows one to program the computer more readily to act like a human tutor. (The word "tutor" is used because it refers to a one-to-one relationship between student and tutor, whereas the word *teacher* can refer to a many-to-one relationship.) Professionals in the field do not agree on the definition of ICBI. This may be due to the fact that many branching programs are responsive and also excellent teaching tools.

Conventional and ICBI possess similar characteristics, but differ in degree. These characteristics can be divided into two categories: characteristics related to the teaching *function* of CBI, and characteristics related to the *structure* of the CBI program. Table 1.1 gives some dimensions of CBI related to the teaching function. A CBI program is more or less intelligent along each of the functional dimensions presented in Table 1.1. It is desirable to design as intelligent CBI as possible, and to purchase CBI that is intelligent in some ways, to the limits of your resources.

ICBI Systems. Presently, there are thousands of branching CBI programs in use. In contrast, only about 25 ICBI programs have been developed, nine of these by the military (Fletcher, in press). As Fletcher notes, his 1975 list contained six ICBI systems, and the 1985 list contained 16.

Examples of ICBI systems include SOPHIE (Brown, Burton, & deKleer, 1982), STEAMER (Hollan, Hutchins, & Weitzman, 1984), and GUIDON (Clancey, 1983). SOPHIE teaches electronic troubleshooting using simulations of electronic faults which the student diagnoses. SOPHIE understands natural language, and the SOPHIE teacher can explain how the student solves problems. STEAMER teaches naval engineering officers to operate steam propulsion systems. The graphic (and intelligent) representation of the dials, controls, and water flow through the system is an innovative feature of STEAMER (Fletcher, in press). GUIDON teaches medical diag-

TABLE 1.1 Functional Intelligence in CBI

Dimension	Level of Intelligence	
	Low	High
Instructional strategy		
Teaching style	Repetitive drill and practice	System shapes student responses and moves student to generalization exercises: method of advancement depends on student response patterns
Amount of interaction	Little interaction	Frequent interaction which begins early in lesson
Course content	Only simple content	Simple and advanced content
Student data (student "model")	Simple model based only on the student's most recent answer	Complex model based on student's response patterns
	No performance records kept	Detailed performance records kept; student progress toward goal presented visually
Student–computer dialogue	Student input accepted only on practice or test items	Student input accepted any time, student and tutor ask and answer questions
Control of instructional sequence	System presents linear sequence, same sequence to each student	Student can request certain sequence or choose the system selected sequence
Evaluation of student input	System evaluates only a one-letter answer	System understands the sense of a student's answer
Feedback to student	Canned feedback No prescriptive advice	Tailored feedback System gives advice based on student's response pattern

nosis by simulating patients with different medical problems. GUIDON can engage in practice doctor–patient dialogues with medical students.

ICBI Teaching Style. In particular, three dimensions of CBI are important in determining intelligence in a CBI system: intelligent diagnosis of error patterns; intelligent feedback, and intelligent dialogue between computer and student. These components of intelligent teaching style are described below.

The first component of ICBI teaching style is *diagnosis of student competencies and errors.* ICBI can diagnose student competencies and errors in several ways. It can adapt to pretest performance by allowing the student to skip material previously learned. It can include a pretest of ability or learning style, and present instruction which will capitalize on the student's preferred way to learn. Finally, ICBI may adapt to scores gathered during instruction, which illuminate error patterns in a student's responses.

The research on learning styles has attempted to categorize learning styles and suggest how instruction may be designed to capitalize on the student's individual style. However, designing ICBI based on a student's learning style is difficult because of assumptions that must be made. This line of research assumes that a student will always make the same type of errors in any lesson. Based on that assumption, a pretest to measure learning style, given even before the student has had a chance with the new material, would be helpful in determining how the lesson should be presented. Learning-style research suggests that students respond relatively independent of the material.

More commonly, however, ICBI is designed to remediate error patterns that occur during the lesson. The system keeps track of student errors, matches error patterns to patterns in its data base, selects the error pattern that most closely matches the student's and provides remedial help aimed at overcoming that particular error. (The computer thus demonstrates insight.) For example, the math student may consistently forget to subtract 1 from a number from which he or she has borrowed (e.g., $32 - 19 = 23$). An ICBI system provides specialized feedback for that problem and extra coaching as necessary. An "unintelligent" system would simply respond "incorrect, please try again" without demonstrating insight as described above.

The second component of ICBI teaching style is the *feedback* presented to overcome student errors. Many instructional variables can be changed in response to student performance to provide a good fit between material and performance. These instructional variables include the type of hints given, number of practice items presented during the lesson before the lesson test, number of illustrative examples presented per new concept, difficulty of instruction, step size, and amount of remedial help. For example, the system may find that one student typically passes posttests after three practice exercises, but another student performs better with five. The system could advise each student on how to increase his or her own individual probability of success based on these data.

ICBI may also adapt instruction based on how the student's response patterns compare to patterns of previous students. This ICBI would draw from an experimental data base that contains information about other students who have taken the course and how they progressed in relation to adaptations they received. ICBI, which has this capability, may constantly improve itself as more and more student progress data are collected.

The third characteristic of ICBI is *intelligent student–computer dialogue*. One important characteristic of ICBI is the ease with which the computer and student communicate with each other. A very intelligent system allows the student to query the computer any time during the lesson. This is done in a manner that is similar to the way a student could query a human instructor during a lesson. A student query could be made with a simple HELP function that allows a student to press a specific key if help is needed, or a query could be made by the student typing in the request. Such CBI employs *natural language* dialogue, which means that student and computer respond to each other in English sentences.

An unintelligent system restricts the student to answering every question with a word, phrase, or statement. CBI intelligence increases as the student is allowed the choice to answer questions with questions or other statements, as in a student–human teacher conversation. For example, a teacher may ask a student "How do you convert Fahrenheit degrees to Celsius?" With a human teacher, a student can give the correct answer, or an incorrect answer, or can also say "I remember that something gets added, but I can't remember the number" or "Will you please repeat the question?" Students are not constrained to picking one answer out of a list of three or four answers as they might be when working with unintelligent CBI.

Student–computer dialogue does not have to be limited to menus or short lists of choices, although this is the most common form of interaction. Natural language technology is far from being widely available, and even research efforts are still in early stages. At the same time, natural language dialogues can be a burden to students who would be required to type in their part of the dialogue. Selecting a choice from a menu requires far less effort.

Figure 1.3 illustrates the student–computer dialogue used in a prototype ICBI module developed by the author (and programmed by Michael Blanks and David Canody of Science Applications International Corporation). The ICBI module allows students to practice problem solving in a military situation. Notice that the interface design includes multiple windows (separate sections of the screen) with lists of items that the student can select. Notice that the student can request help at any time, thus adding flexibility to the dialogue.

Natural language capability (or at least flexible menu choices)

(1) INSTRUCTIONS
Welcome to the SAIC Smart Tutor. Today you will be solving problems in your role as Division Intelligence Officer. The Tutor will evaluate your responses on each problem. See if your answers improve as you go.

(2) PROBLEM #1
What is the value for (ENEMY-TROOPS SIZE)?

(3) INFORMATION	SOLVE PROBLEM	HELP	(4) SELECTED INFORMATION
AIR-DEFENSE DISTRIBUTION AIR-DEFENSE LOCATION AIR-DEFENSE MOVEMENT AIR-SITUATION SUPERIORITY AIR-SITUATION VISIBILITY ARTILLERY SUPPORT			ARTILLERY SUPPORT 5 TO 8 KM (.8 1.0)

(5) CHOICES OF ANSWERS	(6) EVALUATION
Small Large Medium Can't Tell Don't Understand This Problem	You chose SMALL, but the correct answer is LARGE You asked for 1 piece of irrelevant info: ARTY SUPPORT You did not ask for the relevant info: ARMOR NUMBER Time Spent on Problem: 00:01:38

CLICK OUTSIDE EVALUATION WINDOW TO CONTINUE

Figure 1.3. Flexible student–computer dialogue in an ICBI module.

promotes ICBI which incorporates *discovery learning* (also called *Socratic learning*) (Sleeman & Brown, 1982) as opposed to learning the information as it has been programmed, sequenced, and presented on the screen. In discovery learning the student is led through a conversation designed so that the student figures out new information. The computer talks to the student in the way a consultant or private tutor would, rather than engaging in a more sequenced, didactic conversation. In this type of ICBI, the program must adapt according to a complex of variables concerning the student's statements and questions, and continue probing the student (as opposed to presenting information and quizzing) to lead him or her to consider important factors about the topic at hand.

Dialogue intelligence is not limited to natural language dialogue. To increase the intelligence of student–computer dialogue with menus, a designer can add choices to the answer menu that allow the student to respond with something other than an answer. For

TABLE 1.2 Dimensions of Structural Intelligence in CBI

Dimension	Level of Intelligence	
	Low	**High**
Course content	Content embedded in the courseware program	Content programmed in its own knowledge base
Instructional strategy	Strategy embedded in the courseware program	Strategy programmed in its own rule base; system generates instruction and tests based on rules
Student model (or "file")	No student file, or a simple one embedded in the courseware	Student file includes diagnosis and prescriptive advice generated by instructional strategy rule base
Feedback to student	Simple, one word	Tailored feedback created according to rules in instructional strategy rule base
Graphics	Line drawings	Three-dimensional dynamic simulation
Speech	No speech capability	System speaks to students and recognizes speech input

example, a designer could add "Help, please give me another example," "Please repeat the question," or "I'm lost." Choices such as these increase the likelihood that a student will respond to the computer as he or she might to a human teacher.

ICBI Structure. The structure of ICBI includes a three-part program and the computer system's capabilities for feedback, graphics, and speech. As with functional intelligence, the structure of ICBI demonstrates more or less intelligence on several dimensions. Table 1.2 presents dimensions of ICBI structural intelligence.

ICBI is programmed in three components, in contrast to the single-component program in conventional CBI. The components are the course content, the instructional strategy, and the student file. These components are pictured in Figure 1.4.

The *course content* is programmed in one of two formats: as a collection of IF–THEN rules, or in a concept hierarchy (or "semantic") network. Use of IF–THEN rules is more suited when teaching conditions and procedural knowledge such as diagnosis, whereas

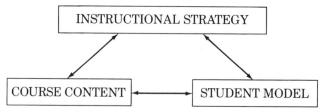

Figure 1.4. ICBI structural components.

networks are useful when teaching equipment operation and maintenance (Fletcher, in press).

An artificial intelligence programming language such as LISP allows for the creation of IF–THEN rule bases. The subject matter is accessed as a flexible language rather than as an invariant sequence of facts as it might be if programmed conventionally. For example, in a lesson about weather, one rule might be "If it is northern Italy, and it is cloudy, and it is November through February, then it will rain."

A semantic network contains nodes and links that represent objects and their relationships. Networks are thus spatially oriented and IF–THEN rule bases more verbally oriented (Fletcher, in press). Networks are usually hierarchically structured.

The *teaching strategy* contains rules or directions about what instruction to present next, dependent on responses in the student file, and it keeps track of how much subject matter is mastered. Teaching strategy modules can be programmed as rules, such as "If two errors are made, present a simpler topic" or "If the answer is correct, advance to the next more difficult topic." The challenging process of translating course content and instructional strategy into rules or hierarchies is called *knowledge engineering*.

The *student file* records and saves student responses. (The student file may also be called a student *model*. All the data on student responses represent or model the student.) From these data, the system deciphers error patterns in the student's responding. The rules for determining error patterns are stored in the instructional strategy rule base. Even more intelligent are ICBI systems that can test their own diagnoses. For example, the system would determine the student's error pattern, predict the next error (and not tell the student), and see if the student actually made that error. In this way, the system could test itself to see how well it "knew" the student, to make sure that it was giving the most helpful feedback possible.

Structural intelligence in ICBI programs has one major benefit that is not seen by the student. Changes to an instructional program are more easily made when an artificial intelligence language is used than if a traditional programming language is used. This is because the subject matter, student file, and teaching strategy are programmed as separate modules. A change in one rule somewhere does not create the rippling effect that changes in conventional programs create.

Exploitation of ICBI. What is the instructional advantage of using ICBI? Who should be considering ICBI? First, ICBI seems most suited for teaching problem solving. Most ICBI is designed for adult students (university, industry, or military), although there are some well-known ICBI programs for children. A well-known ICBI program called WEST teaches arithmetic problem solving in a game format for elementary school children (Burton & Brown, 1982). An ICBI geometry tutor was used and evaluated against traditional instruction in the Pittsburgh public schools over the 1986–1987 year, but evaluation results were not available as of this writing; an ICBI algebra tutor will begin evaluation in the 1987–1988 school year, also in Pittsburgh (F. Boyle, personal communication, September 14, 1987).

Second, ICBI could be considered when the amount of training time available must be held constant or shortened, while at the same time even more content must be learned. This is a common situation in our increasingly complex society. Just because we have more to learn does not mean that we can spend more time in training. The society needs efficient training methods; perhaps an intelligent personal tutor could do the job.

Another justification for ICBI is when the learning levels of expected students are low, or lower than those of previous classes of students. One might expect that special tutoring would improve the progress of these students. Increased tutorial expertise (e.g., increased sensitivity to student responses, ease in student–computer conversation) may be able to bring these students to mastery faster than conventional CBI methods.

Training Simulations

Training simulations in CBI are scenarios of real-life situations that are unveiled as frames progress. Participants act in the simulations, by entering answers, directions, or decisions into the computer, and solve problems. Simulations are usually suited for advanced students who have obtained mastery on a set of concepts and are now ready to apply the knowledge.

Reinforcement is often delayed in simulations. Simulations often employ time compression, and in less than a real-time day a participant might act in a scenario that spans many days worth of simulation activity. Small-scale simulations can be designed for children if the situations are easy and of short duration.

In many simulations, desirable participant action sequences are already known by the computer. Participants may receive computer-generated qualitative assessments of their actions, but better yet, the participant's actions produce natural consequences. Incorrect or inefficient actions produce problems in the scenario, and correct actions produce cost- or time-effective solutions.

A different type of simulation provides training not on quality or correctness of action, but on action structure. An example of such a simulation, which exists only in prototype, is the Yugoslav Dilemma (Swezey, Streufert, Criswell, Unger, & Van Rijn, 1984). The Yugoslav Dilemma presents a 7-day international, military–political crisis scenario, which participants work on in less than a day. The Yugoslav Dilemma scenario never resolves; that is, war is not possible, summits or visits may be arranged, but new problems keep developing. The computer collects information on the speed and complexity or interrelatedness of the participant's action. Certain general action patterns have been hypothesized as effective in these demanding situations, and these patterns may guide future training in the area of crisis-situation behavior (Streufert & Swezey, 1986). This type of simulation may be useful in teaching behavior in complex situations that demand creative rather than textbook solutions.

Instructional Games

Instructional games are a type of training simulation. Like simulations, they require the student to act in a problem situation. Games, however, usually involve fantastic or fanciful situations, whereas many training simulations involve real-life problem situations. The excitement and interest that video arcade computer games generate can teach CBI designers about maintaining student motivation using computer-based instructional games. An interesting game presents a challenge to the player, and the student tries to make progress toward a goal by amassing points or beating previous scores. Computer color graphics also foster interest. Games allow for discovery learning; the actual results of a player's own actions teach and strengthen performance. Such enormously popular techniques have not been part of school curricula in the past. One influential educator has stated that anyone who uses [a computer] to do anything that isn't fun should be tried for a felony (Lindsley, 1982).

Figure 1.5 presents a game format used by the Merrill Lynch Training Division that is popular with account executive trainees. The object of this game is to answer enough drill and practice questions to obtain bonus points. Enough points will place the trainee's name in a Hall of Fame.

Training Simulators

A computerized training simulator is a replica of a piece of equipment that is used to teach students how to operate or repair the actual equipment. A training simulator provides an opportunity for the student to practice operation and repair skills that have been introduced by lecture, film, or textbook. Some simulators keep student performance records and print out student performance data for past as well as present sessions. Some simulators contain a student workstation with computer for introduction of new material using CBI. A simulation is flat, delivered on a computer video monitor, and a simulator is three-dimensional.

A computerized training simulator resembles the actual equipment to some degree of fidelity between low and high. A low-fidelity simulator may not look like the actual equipment and have low *physical* fidelity, but may function like it in some way and contain high *functional* fidelity. A high-fidelity simulator possesses high physical and functional fidelity and looks and acts like the actual equipment. Clever simulator design incorporates as low a level of fidelity as possible, thus keeping down dollar costs without sacrificing training-effectiveness. The research on fidelity and simulators is discussed in detail in Hays and Singer (in press).

A recent experiment assessed the effects of degree (i.e., high, medium, and low) of physical and functional fidelity on training effectiveness (Allen, Hays, & Buffardi, 1986). The simulator used was for training troubleshooting of a piece of equipment developed for experimental purposes. The equipment contained 28 electromechanical relays and five solid-state pull-up panels interconnected to eight output devices (e.g., water pump, fan). Figure 1.6 shows the three degrees of physical fidelity used in the experiment. The high-physical-fidelity system was the actual equipment. The medium-physical-fidelity simulator duplicated half of the high-fidelity components, and the low-physical-fidelity simulator was only a symbolic representation of the high-physical-fidelity simulator. The high-functional-fidelity simulator provided information about the states of components and output devices. The medium-functional-fidelity simulator provided information only about components. The low-functional-fidelity simulator provided no information. The data

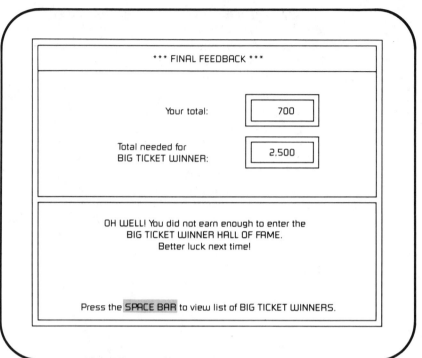

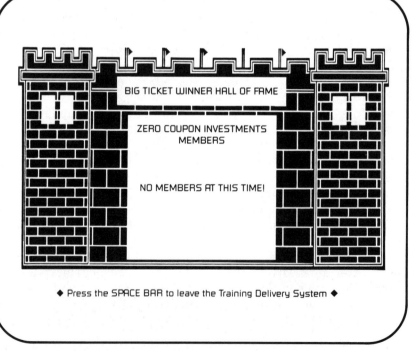

Figure 1.5. Instructional game format (courtesy of Catherine M. Taggart, Merrill Lynch Training Technologies).

Figure 1.6. High-, medium-, and low-physical-fidelity simulators used in Allen, Hays, and Buffardi (1986; photos courtesy of John Allen, George Mason University).

showed that training effectiveness increases with fidelity, and that low functional fidelity was associated with slowest times to solution.

Flight simulators are high-fidelity replicas of a cockpit; they look like actual cockpits, employ sound effects, some even bounce around on their platforms, and the CBI practice programs create simulated real-life flight situations which respond to the student pilot's actions. Through use of computer graphics, the student may view the changes in sky and ground below as he or she manipulates the controls. The computer also provides consequences such as instrument readings and target distances for the student's actions. Often, practice in these highly sophisticated simulators follows mastery of basic concepts and operations taught in less expensive ways.

Another example of an experimental high-fidelity simulator is the AMTESS (Army Maintenance Test and Evaluation Simulation System) devices, used for conducting research in simulation and training in automotive engine repair (Criswell, Swezey, Allen, & Hays, 1984). The simulators have been developed under the auspices of the U.S. Army Research Institute for the Behavioral and Social Sciences. They employ a computer and student terminal for delivery of instruction and a three-dimensional replica of an engine for practice in the engine repair skills being taught. The computer assesses the accuracy of manipulation on the engine by means of sensors attached to numerous parts of the engine. Designing courseware for these devices is challenging because task analyses are complex, programming for teaching each subtask must consider the performance level attained for each component skill, and student learning histories vary.

Expert Systems

Expert systems consist of two components: a data base and a decision-making capability. Expert systems are designed for use in situations where it is difficult for human beings to make good decisions. Examples of these situations include times when quick, important decisions are needed, or cases where a large amount of information must be systematically studied and weighed. In both cases, the systems help people in situations where they might be prone to make mistakes. These situations could range from exciting, fast-paced, even dangerous, to repetitive and boring situations—all cases where people might make mistakes.

Expert systems may be used in training, to compare a student's decisions to the decision of the system. Expert systems in these cases function more as training aids and do not deliver instruction.

What is interesting about expert systems is the way in which the computer is programmed to make decisions as a person would. One way is based on *multiattribute utilities analysis*. To decipher how an expert human being makes decisions, the system designer asks experts in the field (whatever field the system is being designed for) to specify all the aspects or dimensions he or she would consider important in making the decision, assign a number value or weight to indicate the relative importance of each dimension, then compute a score for several different courses of action. The decision or course of action receiving the highest score is the one recommended by the system.

A second way that expert systems make decisions is by comparison. The expert system is filled with outcomes of previous decisions. The system (or the user) matches the present circumstances with past ones and makes a decision based on the quality of previous outcomes. To the extent that present circumstances match past ones, the decision of the system is "certain" or "reliable." Many systems calculate a coefficient of certainty for each decision they yield.

Embedded Training

Computerized *embedded training* is CBI that teaches operation or repair of a system or piece of equipment, but it is embedded in the actual equipment. Embedded training may be preferable to training by simulator (or other means such as textbook) when embedded training would not interfere with normal operations of the equipment. For example, there may be times when the system is not in use and could be used for training during these times. Use of the actual system would be less expensive than developing a simulated system dedicated for use in training. Of course, student performance records and practice exercises must be kept in a data base separate from the "live" data in the system.

Equipment or systems that contain computers are obvious candidates for embedded training. For example, the author and a team of colleagues are designing a computer system that calculates the number of people that would be required to operate and maintain any piece of military equipment (Criswell, Williford, & Smith, 1987). The system design calls for embedded training, so a training module, teaching users how to operate the system, will be included. To access the embedded training, the user will select the "Training" option from the main menu. The main menu and training menus are shown in Figure 1.7.

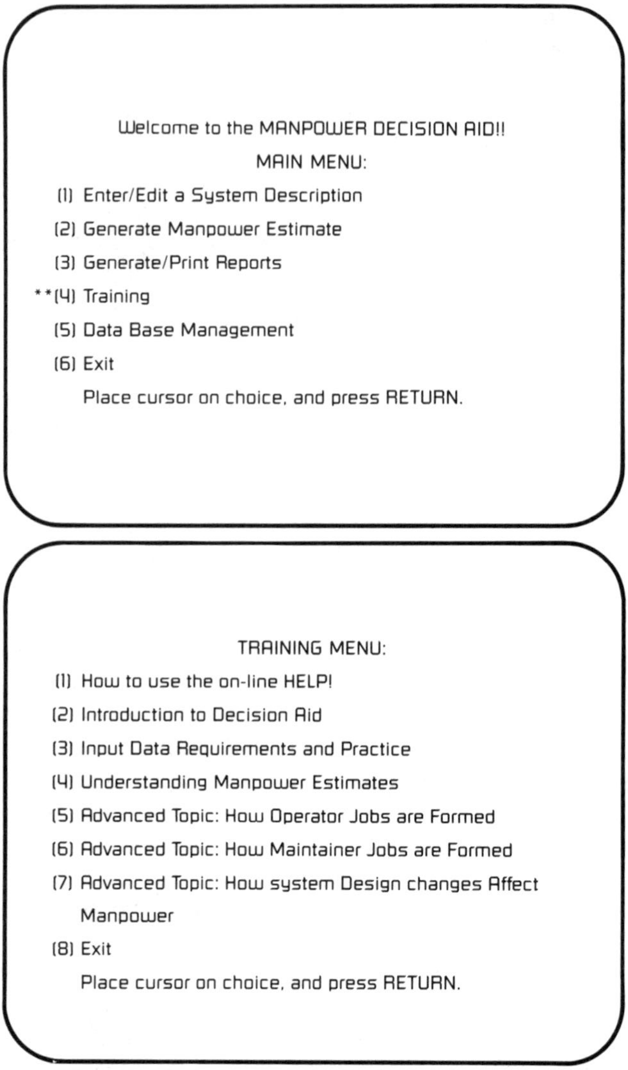

```
Welcome to the MANPOWER DECISION AID!!
               MAIN MENU:
  (1) Enter/Edit a System Description

  (2) Generate Manpower Estimate

  (3) Generate/Print Reports

**(4) Training

  (5) Data Base Management

  (6) Exit

     Place cursor on choice, and press RETURN.
```

```
               TRAINING MENU:
  (1) How to use the on-line HELP!

  (2) Introduction to Decision Aid

  (3) Input Data Requirements and Practice

  (4) Understanding Manpower Estimates

  (5) Advanced Topic: How Operator Jobs are Formed

  (6) Advanced Topic: How Maintainer Jobs are Formed

  (7) Advanced Topic: How system Design changes Affect
      Manpower

  (8) Exit

     Place cursor on choice, and press RETURN.
```

Figure 1.7. Main menu and embedded training menu (from Criswell, Williford, & Smith, 1987).

Adaptive CBI Testing

Assessment, practice without feedback, is an important part of tutorials and ICBI because it measures how well a student is performing relative to the goal. Adaptive CBI testing is a recent advance. Adaptive CBI testing determines on-line both the number and difficulty of test items to be administered in order to test adequately the student's performance level using a minimum number of items. In nonadaptive testing, all students receive the same items. Studies have shown that adaptive CBI testing as opposed to nonadaptive testing can substantially reduce the number of items administered, and save large amounts of testing time, without loss in precision (D. J. Weiss, 1979). This type of testing has been developed to screen military recruits, where reductions in testing time can result in significant financial savings (Pliske, Gade, & Johnson, 1984; Sands & Gade, 1983).

Computer-Managed Instruction

Computer-managed instruction (CMI) is included in some CBI systems. Important functions of CMI include: selecting instructional and test material for individual students, scheduling instruction, testing and record keeping, providing advice to students, controlling the quality of instruction, and providing support for educational research (Pennypacker, 1978). Testing and record keeping are found in good CBI systems. A CMI system can allow a student to register for a course, keep track of daily progress, and begin each session where the last one ended. A student can receive a daily printout of his or her performance record from many CMI systems. The system can assign extra work if needed. A CMI system can also provide progress summaries for the human instructor. Tracks of student progress are important in evaluating teaching techniques.

Hardware and Software Considerations in CBI

Since the 1960s, advances in computer hardware have taken place at a rapid pace, and very powerful computers are widely available in schools and in private homes. This burgeoning has happened primarily in the United States, but has occurred in other countries as well. Development of high-quality instructional programs, however, has lagged far behind developments in hardware and programming languages. The gap is widely lamented in the United States (e.g., Bork, 1984), but it appears to be even wider in other countries (Zinn, 1981). There is an enormous need for the development of quality courseware in a wide range of subject matter, for schools, universities, government, business, industrial, and military training programs.

Hardware and programming languages are obviously important

in CBI, but only to the extent that they provide a vehicle for the courseware. *Human factors* is a term that describes the relation of person and machine, the human elements involved in systems that use machines or other inanimate objects. Another term, *man–machine interface*, refers to the points of contact between person and machine. Human factors in CBI refers to the way in which computers, computer screens, and video monitor displays are designed to maximize their effective use by the people most likely to use them.

Computer manufacturers have made available a large number of interesting features that may be used in delivering the courseware. In each case, however, the feature should be assessed for its instructional value and its proper implementation—its worth relative to human use and gain.

For example, on some computers, the student may answer a multiple-choice question by typing the letter of the desired choice. But on computers with a touch-screen feature, the student need only touch the desired answer. The finger breaks a photocell that triggers the computer's next frame. A touch screen, now widely available, is a feature that makes easier a student's physical interaction with the computer. The touch screen increases the system's *transparency*. Transparency permits the student to concentrate on the lesson without being distracted by computer operating procedures, and is a desirable feature. However, touch screens are unimportant if the course is poorly designed or if merely touching an answer does not provide relevant interaction with the material.

Split screens (a single frame that presents diverse information in separate sections or *windows* of the screen) are another computer capability that eases student–computer interaction. Use of split screens may reduce memory demands on the student, as well as prevent the student from having to page back to review previous screens. Poorly designed split screens, however, may present a bewildering and complex appearance. Split screens with poorly sequenced instruction will probably hinder learning.

Color graphics is another capability that does not in and of itself improve learning. As with the features described above, color graphics can be unclear and confusing. On the other hand, color graphics and good courseware could, if well designed, create an interesting and effective course.

Software plays an important role in CBI. The software should provide reliable access to the course. For example, the software should allow a student to recover quickly from a typographical error. The software should function quickly. The software should allow the student to progress easily through the course.

The purpose of CBI is to facilitate learning. The vehicle for this is a program or sequence of instruction that accomplishes clearly specified objectives that have been carefully considered and which are integrated into a total educational program. Computers improve the delivery of instruction, but they do not accomplish instruction without good courseware.

Can computer features override poorly designed instruction? Yes and no. Yes, especially if one considers the motivational aspects of CBI. CBI can be different and colorful. Computer games can be fun. But no, if good programs of instruction and computer capabilities are poorly integrated. And no, if what CBI accomplishes is not what we desire.

What makes courseware effective? At the very least, courseware should be designed around important learning principles. Some of these principles are discussed in later chapters. These include use of clear instructional objectives, careful overall and detailed sequencing, frequent opportunities for student practice, and appropriate consequences delivered by the computer. In addition, each screen should be carefully laid out to ease the interaction between student and computer. Finally, the courseware should hold attention and maintain motivation.

In summary, CBI can be effective, or it can waste a student's time. Instruction in any medium (e.g., human lecture, textbook, films, television) has the same potential. The success of CBI lies in exploiting the capabilities of instructional designers (psychologists and educators), computer designers and programmers, and graphics designers. Each area of expertise contributes to better CBI.

Study Questions

Study questions are provided at the end of each chapter. The questions cover the important points in the chapter. There are two types of questions: definition and discussion. A definition question requires a short answer that comes directly from the text. A discussion question requires an answer that may include synthesis of the material in the text. Your learning of the material will probably be different if you answer the questions by referring back to the text than if you do not look back. It may take a couple of hours for you to write the answers or to make notes about the answers. You might also want to answer these questions orally, alone or in class. You may find that reviewing these questions periodically will help you maintain mastery of the material. You and your instructor may determine how best to use these questions.

Definition Questions

1. Define *computer-based instruction* (CBI).
2. List and define the three physical components required to implement CBI.
3. How are linear and branching tutorials alike, and how are they different?
4. Describe the four components of successful teaching described by Skinner (1984).
5. Describe the 10 specific steps in the teaching process described by Becker, Englemann, and Thomas.
6. What is a natural language query?
7. What is an expert system? What are two ways in which expert systems make decisions?
8. Define *simulation* and *simulator*.
9. How are simulations and simulators alike, and how are they different?
10. What is the difference between standard and adaptive testing?
11. List some important functions of computer-managed instruction.

Discussion Questions

1. How should CBI be used in relation to other class materials?
2. Describe the societal and psychological influences that led to the rise of CBI. Will CBI continue to grow in importance? Why?
3. Why is *intelligent* CBI difficult to define?
4. How might drill and practice programs be used effectively in classrooms?
5. How are computer games instructional? How might they be used effectively in classrooms?
6. How should you determine the level of physical and functional fidelity that a training simulator should have?
7. Should the capabilities of available hardware dictate courseware design? Why?
8. In general, what makes courseware effective?

CHAPTER 2

Structural and Functional Approaches to CBI Design

The main topics of this chapter are:

- *The science of human learning*
- *The structural approach to the study of learning*
- *The functional approach to the study of learning*
- *An integrated approach to CBI design*

Introduction

Behind the design of any instructional techniques are principles of learning. Learning may be defined as a relatively enduring change in behavior caused by environmental events. Learning principles describe this change. The psychological processes involved in learning are systematic and orderly, and an understanding of those processes is important for anyone who designs instruction. The goal of instruction is to cause students to change or learn. Thus, designing CBI calls for an understanding of principles of learning.

Is CBI design science or art? "Both" is the right answer. The science in CBI design involves sequencing instructional events that facilitate learning as well as determining the best content of those events. Art in CBI design involves such things as developing tasteful displays, attention-grabbing language, and interesting content. You will find CBI designers who revolt against either the science or art of CBI design. From those who think that CBI design is an art comes the notion that a CBI designer need only create meaningful experiences that touch the souls of students. From those who think that CBI design is all science comes the view that properly laid out instructional sequences that play to a student's mental abilities are all you need in effective courseware. This book is admittedly biased toward the science of learning and how it translates into good CBI. But every lesson is different, and designer imagination in application of the science is generally required to produce good CBI.

Principles of learning describe all sorts of changes in what a person knows and does, including academic work, social interaction, and physical skills such as bike riding. Learning is not confined to improvements in behavior. Misbehavior and mistakes are also learned according to the same principles.

Learning may be described from two scientific viewpoints: structural and functional. A *structural* viewpoint describes what and when learning occurs, and a *functional* perspective describes under what conditions learning occurs. Historically, psychologists have been in conflict with each other over which perspective best describes behavior and what causes people to learn.

The structural perspective emphasizes learning at a point in time. Cognitive psychology is often associated with a structural viewpoint. In addition, many child and developmental psychologists, notably those who describe stages of development, support structural viewpoints. Structuralists tell us what most people do. Some structural psychologists hypothesize how brain activity (obviously not visible) may cause learning and behavior. This has led some (e.g., Fredericksen, 1984) to discuss how teaching should be designed based on hypothesized brain activity. Short-term memory is seen as placing bounds on the amount of information that a person can handle. One structural technique involves grouping or chunking together pieces of information. Chunking enables a student to absorb more into the short-term-memory area of the brain than if many, perhaps unrelated, pieces of information are presented singly.

In contrast, a functional viewpoint describes why learning occurs the way it does, under what conditions learning occurs, and how learning is caused. The functional perspective emphasizes the description of actual—as opposed to hypothesized—factors which control transitions and the sequence of learning. Behavioral psychology is often associated with a functional viewpoint. These psychologists try to uncover the causes of learning, rather than describe the structure of learning. Functionalists attempt to tell us why people do what they do. These psychologists maintain that events in one's external environment, often visible, are powerful causes of behavior, and that it is therefore unnecessary, and even counterproductive, to spend time speculating about the role of brain activity in learning. People have for years been designing teaching procedures. The procedures used to design instruction all include careful attention to the sequencing of environmental events. These events include the manner in which material is presented and the manner in which consequences are delivered to the student.

A state of concurrence actually exists, however, because both structural and functional viewpoints are necessary in designing instruction. The structural orientation can suggest what to teach. For example, structural information suggests that people of certain ages or abilities accept or absorb and use information. From a functional viewpoint, however, we learn how to arrange instructional events so that learning occurs. In addition, we may cause students to learn despite structural norms or predictions.

In many cases, it is possible to explain with both perspectives why any one teaching procedure causes learning. For example, chunking may be said to enhance learning because the brain more readily accepts chunks than unrelated material. It may also be said that chunking is effective because contextually related material is a powerful instructional stimulus. Deciding on which explanation of chunking you like depends on what question you are asking. Using an analogy to computers, which better explains how computers operate: electron flow or applications programs? Either answer is arguable; selecting both is fuller.

Gollin (1970) addressed the notions of structural and functional descriptions of behavior. First, he states that the learning domain should be defined: How does learning develop for any student? For example, what math problems can most sixth-grade students solve? Next, ways to alter that domain should be sought. How might we expand that domain? Can we teach the typical math problems, and even some more? The two perspectives are discussed in more detail in the following sections.

The Structural Perspective

Basic Paradigm

Cognitive psychology exemplifies the structural perspective. Cognitive psychology describes learning in terms of human information processing, as shown in Figure 2.1. Stimulation or information from the environment is input into the sensory register of the brain. Mental activities taking place in the brain of the recipient of the input include pattern recognition, short-term memory, and long-term memory. Input is encoded and stored in the brain in short-term or long-term memory. Some cognitive scientists refer to executive control processes that direct or influence input and output.

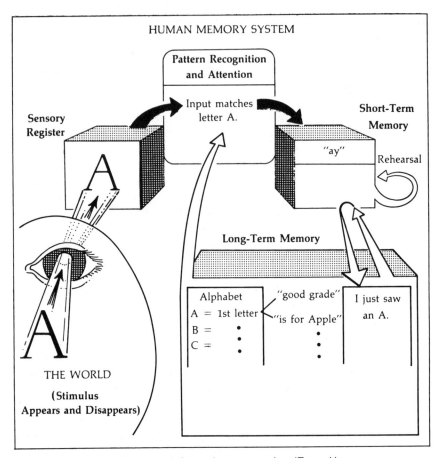

Figure 2.1. Model of human information processing (From *Human Memory*, 2/E, by Roberta L. Klatzky. Copyright ©1975, 1980 W.H. Freeman and Company. Reprinted with permission.)

These processes include motivation, selective perception, encoding, memory, and retrieval. These mental processes (which are not directly observable) are the emphasis of cognitive psychology. Output refers to information in short- or long-term memory that is retrieved or reconstructed by the person. Output may be triggered by environmental demands for recognition, recall, and physical action.

Perhaps the cognitive psychology concept most important to instructional design is memory. Based on scientific studies, memory specialists suggest several techniques that may be used to increase memory: paying attention to input, repeating to yourself or rehearsing what has just been inputted, and organizing input into categories, or *chunks* (Miller, 1956).

Organizing input into easily remembered categories can be facilitated by the use of devices that represent the input. These input devices must be coherent and easily remembered themselves. These devices include coined phrases, acronyms, mental images or mental pictures, invented stories, and rhymes.

Structure of Human Development

A structural perspective emphasizing internal processing is held not only by cognitive psychologists but by many developmental psychologists as well, as mentioned earlier. These developmental psychologists describe stages of human development that relate to age. Many developmental psychologists suggest that as children grow, the ways in which they learn, change.

The exemplary developmental stage psychologist Piaget (1964) developed the theory that children grow intellectually in stages. From years 0 to 2, children explore their tiny environments, and through physical exploration, learn that objects exist and do not change from day to day. This is the sensorimotor stage. This is a period of motor action.

The period from age 2 to 7 years is called the preoperational period by Piaget (1964). During this time, the child learns that a word can stand for, or represent, an object. Thus, using language is an important advance during this period. Children at this level can identify things they see, and they learn what things do by touching them or otherwise directly experiencing them.

Facts about the young child's developmental level should influence design of CBI for children (Chapman, Dollaghan, Kenworthy, & Miller, 1983). Children below the age of 3 can learn to touch a screen to indicate their choices directly, but keyboard entry, even when the keyboard is color coded to the screen, is generally too difficult for children this young. Preschool children engage in fantasy play such as telephoning, playing house, and hiding/running away from monsters, so these activities should be worked into instruction. Activities involving drawing inferences should be avoided. Vocabulary used in instruction should be words that occur frequently in their environments.

Children of age 4 have formed *scripts* (summaries of what usually happens), are surprised when a routine is broken, and can talk about their expectations (Schank & Abelson, 1977). Younger children usually talk about current events. Instruction for these children might emphasize routine events in their lives.

During ages 7 to 12 years, the period of concrete operations, the child learns to act on mental representations. During this time, the child begins to solve problems. The child learns basic mathematical concepts such as add, subtract, multiply, divide, greater than, and less than.

From age 12 to 18 years, many children develop the ability to perform formal operations (Piaget, 1964). Examples of formal operations are deduction or rule following and induction or rule making. A child who can deduce can imagine "What if X happens?" A child may also be able to make guesses or inductions as to why certain events occur.

Adults, from age 18 to 50 or 60, do not pass into new stages of cognitive development, but continue to learn and expand their set of formal operations to meet environmental demands. But after the age of 50 or 60, some people may perform more poorly on skills requiring speed or short-term memory (Birren, Woods, & Williams, 1980). Responsibilities and pressures of adulthood thus both inhibit and enhance learning in older persons.

White (1983) speculates that the spread of computer learning to classes for the very young may change the type of learning accomplished by children of certain ages. For example, by using computer graphics, a child in the preoperational stage may be able to learn about things he can not touch or directly experience. A young child may learn more about objects themselves by operating (e.g., moving, coloring) computer graphic pictures of the objects on the computer screen.

Structural CBI Design

Instructional techniques all linked to cognitive psychology have been described by MacLachlan (1986). The techniques suggest ways to increase memory and to stimulate deep cognitive processes. These are summarized below.

1. Memory is increased when the student is paying attention. Explaining the benefits of the lesson to the student will help capture the student's attention (see Figure 2.2).

2. Precede text with a question about the content to follow, or present only partial information, to stimulate curiosity (see Figure 2.3). The pre-question technique has been associated with double the learning over modules without pre-questions (MacLachlan, 1986). Presenting partial information on the first screen is a technique derived from advertising called a *hot break* which is used in mail-order campaigns to get recipients to turn the page for more information (Nash, 1982, cited in MacLachlan, 1986). Some cognitive psychologists (e.g., Hall, 1983) attribute the effectiveness of these procedures to their ability to stimulate deep cognitive processes.

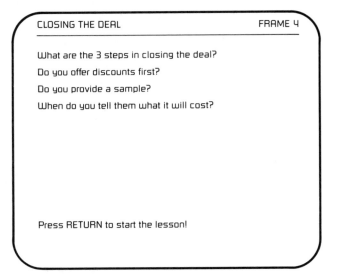

```
┌─────────────────────────────────────────────┐
│  CLOSING THE DEAL                    FRAME 1  │
│  ───────────────────────────────────────────  │
│                                               │
│  One day, you will probably make a big sale   │
│  because of information you will learn in      │
│  this lesson!                                  │
│                                               │
└─────────────────────────────────────────────┘
```

Figure 2.2. Increase attention by explaining benefit.

```
┌─────────────────────────────────────────────┐
│  CLOSING THE DEAL                    FRAME 4  │
│  ───────────────────────────────────────────  │
│                                               │
│  What are the 3 steps in closing the deal?     │
│  Do you offer discounts first?                 │
│  Do you provide a sample?                      │
│  When do you tell them what it will cost?      │
│                                               │
│                                               │
│  Press RETURN to start the lesson!             │
└─────────────────────────────────────────────┘
```

Figure 2.3. Stimulate curiosity with prequestioning.

3. Connect new information thematically to information learned previously, using chronologically ordered narratives to the extent possible, in order to increase memory (see Figure 2.4).

4. Keep information flow high to avoid boredom. Boredom is fostered by use of overly familiar words (such as clichés) and superordinate category nouns (e.g., the word *car* is more apt to bore than

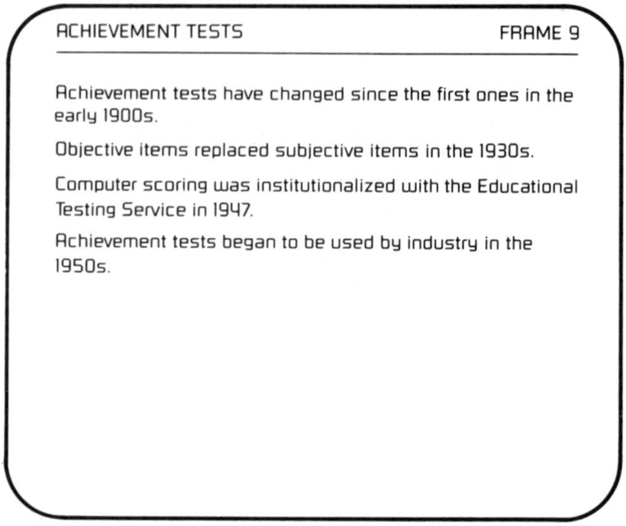

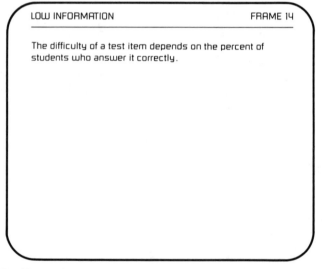

ACHIEVEMENT TESTS   FRAME 9

Achievement tests have changed since the first ones in the early 1900s.

Objective items replaced subjective items in the 1930s.

Computer scoring was institutionalized with the Educational Testing Service in 1947.

Achievement tests began to be used by industry in the 1950s.

Figure 2.4. Link content together with chronological narrative.

LOW INFORMATION   FRAME 14

The difficulty of a test item depends on the percent of students who answer it correctly.

Figure 2.5. Keep information flow high to prevent boredom. This frame contains only a little information.

Rolls-Royce). Use a computer system that presents information at a rapid speed (see Figures 2.5 and 2.6).

5. For information that is difficult to integrate with narrative, provide a mnemonic or a visual aid to increase memory. Vivid pictures increase memory (see Figure 2.7).

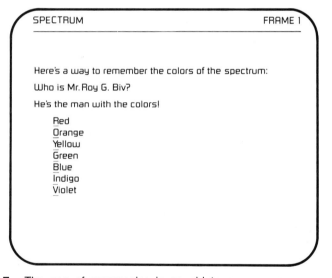

Figure 2.6. This frame contains more information and is less boring than the frame in Figure 2.5.

> SPECTRUM   FRAME 1
> _____
>
> Here's a way to remember the colors of the spectrum:
>
> Who is Mr. Roy G. Biv?
>
> He's the man with the colors!
>
>   Red
>   Orange
>   Yellow
>   Green
>   Blue
>   Indigo
>   Violet

Figure 2.7. The use of mnemonics is an aid to memory.

6. The mind tends to neglect component parts when the total picture is presented. To counter this effect, ask students to draw inferences involving intermediate steps before the entire scenario is presented (see Figure 2.8).

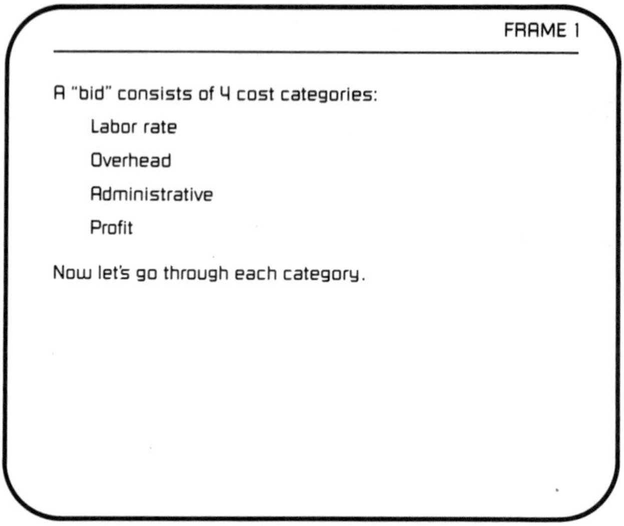

```
                                                    FRAME 1

    A "bid" consists of 4 cost categories:
         Labor rate
         Overhead
         Administrative
         Profit

    Now let's go through each category.
```

Figure 2.8. Emphasis on components is important.

The Functional Perspective

Basic Paradigm

The basic learning paradigm illustrates why learning occurs and is presented in Figure 2.9. This diagram illustrates the very powerful relation between what a person does, the response, and environmental events before it (antecedents) and after it (consequents). As learning occurs, an antecedent event comes to occasion a response. Contingent on the response, a consequence is presented.

This simple relation between the environment and what a person does has profound implications for instructional designers and teachers. If we change the antecedent or consequent stimuli in the environment (the environment being motivational factors and the instructional material), we can change the student's behavior. In the case of CBI, the antecedent and consequent events are contained in the courseware.

It is important to know that the present environment, the instructional material, is not the only thing that helps or hinders a student's learning. Two other factors are involved. One factor is the genetic makeup of the student. Heredity places learning limits on us all. The second factor is the student's past experiences. Past experiences include such things as previous academic achievement, as well as previous success or failure at education. Past experiences

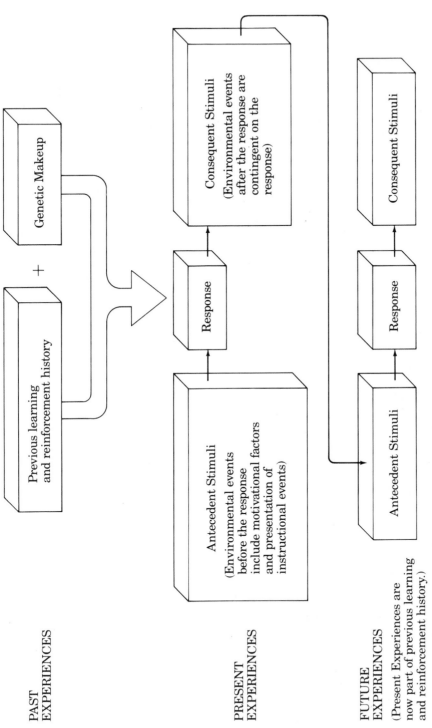

Figure 2.9. Basic learning paradigm.

41

were shaped by the antecedent and consequent events surrounding the student's behavior at those times. Thus all three factors together produce learning.

For purposes of designing instruction, however, present environmental influences are the most important of the three factors. This is because a student enters an instructional program with a genetic makeup and prior experiences already intact. The present conditions are available for teachers to control. We cannot teach everyone to do everything by designing courseware properly. However, we increase teacher (human or computer) effectiveness by designing instruction based on what we know about learning environments.

The simple relation between the environment and behavior forms the basis for designing instruction for both simple and complex behavior. What is learned can be viewed as a complex series of simultaneous and sequential antecedent–behavior–consequent events, where one consequence functions as both a consequence and an antecedent. What has already happened sets the stage for what is to happen next. For example, a student responds with a sum in the units column; completion of this step is the reinforcer and also the antecedent event for going on to sum up the tens column. Teaching a person to type "1" on the computer is merely a less complicated version of teaching a doctor how to diagnose a rare illness. In both cases, antecedent and consequent events have to be arranged to cause the student to learn the desired skill.

At any one time, a variety of antecedent and consequent events are at work in the student's environment. At the time a student is learning, the instructional material immediately before him or her is at work, as well as environmental events in the classroom such as rules regarding conduct, as well as events occurring in the home that affect the student's motivation.

Functional View of Human Development

Psychologists also describe development from a functional viewpoint. Functional psychologists are interested in explaining how the structure of development is acquired. They state that a child's learning is not determined by his age or his personality, but by "species characteristics, biological maturation, or the history of interaction with the particular environment from the moment of conception" (Bijou & Baer, 1978, p. 19). Bijou and Baer make the important point that behavior may be described as an interactional sequence. Behavior affects other behavior. Learning of one thing affects learning of another. This view provides a rich context for the simple antecedent–behavior–consequence sequence.

Functional psychologists, then, do not predict what a person does based solely on age or developmental level. They explain why a person does what he or she does by examining the person's present environment, watching the person to determine what antecedent and consequent events are at work in the environment, and inquiring about the person's previous life experiences. Recommendations about CBI design from a functional perspective will strongly emphasize that individual students learn depending on how they have learned in the past. CBI technology allows for courseware design that is sensitive to numerous students' individual needs.

Functional CBI Design

Instructional techniques linked to behavioral psychology emphasize environmental events involved in the learning process. The remainder of this chapter provides basic guidance for instructional design from the functional perspective.

1. To teach anything, it is important to cause the student's behavior to change by changing events in the environment. The events involved in courseware are presentations of the material with directions on how to respond (antecedent events) and reinforcing events that inform the student about the correctness of the response and set up the next presentation of material (see Figure 2.10).

2. New learning results from frequent responding because the instructional events in the environment must have something to act on in order for learning to occur (see Figure 2.11).

3. Learning progresses from beginner-level responses which are slow and incorrect, to fluent responses which are faster and accurate, to generalized responses which are exhibited in circumstances that were not explicitly taught. Changes in instructional material presentations foster the change from beginner to generalization-level learning (see Figure 2.12).

4. Positive reinforcers encourage continued responding. Positive reinforcers may be contrived (e.g., verbal messages such as "correct") or natural (e.g., student's response results in a completed action). Learning progresses through beginning to generalization levels with a shift from contrived to natural reinforcers (see Figure 2.13).

5. The effects of too many or too harsh error messages ("punishers") can be devastating. If a student's behavior is constantly suppressed, the student will quit responding. The student should be given realistic instructional challenges (see Figure 2.14).

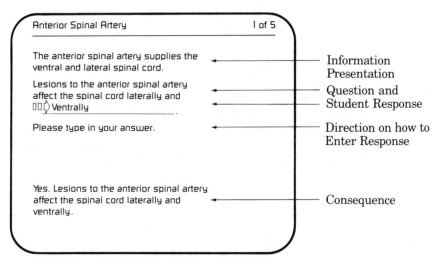

Figure 2.10. Instructional events in CBI.

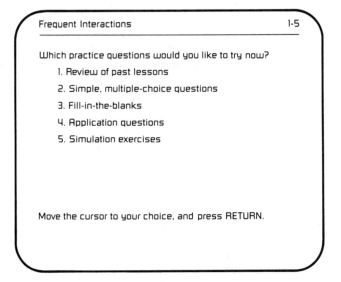

Figure 2.11. CBI provides frequent opportunities for students to respond.

VOCABULARY   Frame A

A martinet demands rigid adherence to rules.

Select the definition of martinet from the following:

  1—Person who rigidly adheres to rules.

  2—Person lives and lets live.

  3—Person who loves Martins.

  4—Person who expects others to live lawful lives.

Frame A:
 Beginner level,
 easy multiple choice
 question

VOCABULARY   Frame B

A M_____ insists that rules be followed.

Type in your answer = _____.

Frame B:
 Beginner level,
 more difficult,
 fill-in-the-blank
 question

VOCABULARY   Frame C

Pretend you're a martinet and a manager.

An employee comes in 20 minutes late because his daughter spilled juice on her dress and he had to change her.

Which would you do?

  1. Sympathize.

  2. Ignore.

  3. Listen.

  4. Praise.

  5. Chastise and dock pay.

Frame C:
 Application/
 Generalization
 Question

Figure 2.12. Progression from beginner- to generalization-level responses.

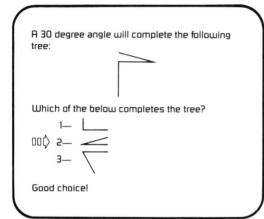

"Good Choice" is a contrived positive reinforcer.

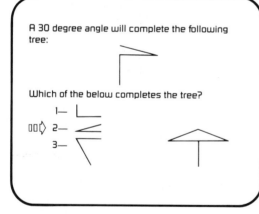

The completed tree is a natural positive reinforcer.

Figure 2.13.   Contrived and natural positive reinforcers.

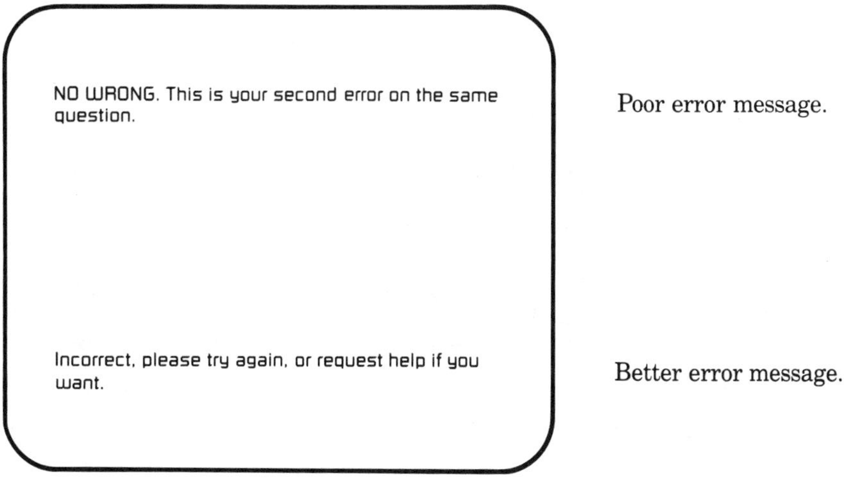

NO WRONG. This is your second error on the same question.

Poor error message.

Incorrect, please try again, or request help if you want.

Better error message.

Figure 2.14. Harsh error messages can be devastating, not at all funny.

An Integrated Approach: Structure and Function in CBI Design

There is little use in designing CBI from either a structuralist or a functionalist viewpoint. The structural approach tells us what people learn and suggests what antecedent events will be effective. The functional approach emphasizes antecedent, but especially consequent events. Overall, the use of both structural and functional viewpoints provides the most effective approach to CBI design. Table 2.1 summarizes the two perspectives.

At present, the functional approach to teaching is more developed than the structural approach; that is, we know more about the teaching process than we do about what exactly to teach and what antecedent materials to use. The functional approach tells instructional designers to sequence instruction, present material, require a response, and present a reinforcer, but designers often use trial and error when designing the material to teach a specific objective.

There is much current interest in structural or cognitive studies. It is clear that a CBI designer or CBI user should understand how people learn and how antecedent and consequent events are arranged to shape behavior and foster generalization. And because instructional material is so heavily oriented toward antecedent events, it is also important to know what are the effective configurations of antecedent events.

TABLE 2.1 Summary of Structural and Functional Approaches

	Approaches	
Dimensions	**Structural/Cognitive**	**Functional/Behavioral**
Basic paradigm	Emphasis on brain activity	Emphasis on environmental events
View of human development	Normative, emphasizes point in time	Individual, emphasizes history
CBI design	CBI instructional events should increase memory and stimulate cognitive processes	CBI instructional events should present information, require frequent responses, and provide meaningful contingent consequences

Suggestions that functionalists have outlived their usefulness and that structural knowledge is sufficient to design CBI are misguided. Equally foolish is a position that holds that understanding the learning process is all that is required to design effective, economical CBI. An integrated approach to CBI design combines information about the learning process with information about presentation of antecedent events, thus capturing the usefulness of both perspectives.

Study Questions

Definition Questions

1. What is the emphasis of a structural view of learning?
2. What is the emphasis of a functional view of learning?
3. How is learning structured, according to cognitive psychology?
4. Briefly, how does the structure of learning change throughout the life span?
5. What is the basic learning paradigm, according to a functional view?
6. How does a functionalist view human development?
7. How does courseware fulfill the functions of environmental events in the basic learning paradigm?
8. How generally can we explain complex learning using the simple learning paradigm?

Discussion Questions

1. Can a person learn a wrong answer? How? Can a student learn to misbehave in class? How?
2. Why are structural and functional views of learning important in the design of CBI?
3. What mistakes could a CBI designer make if he or she designed a course from a purely structural viewpoint? from a purely functional viewpoint?

CHAPTER 3

CBI Design, Production, and Evaluation

The main topics of this chapter are:

* *A 10-step process used to design, produce, and evaluate CBI:*

Step 1: Conduct environmental analysis

Step 2: Conduct knowledge engineering

Step 3: Establish goals and instructional objectives

Step 4: Sequence topics and tasks

Step 5: Write courseware

Step 6: Design each frame

Step 7: Program the computer

Step 8: Produce accompanying documents

Step 9: Evaluate and revise the CBI

Step 10: Implement and follow-up

* *CBI design as a collaborative process*

Introduction

The process of designing, producing, and testing CBI may be seen in 10 steps. Although deadlines and available money usually determine the depth to which each step is considered, the same 10 steps should be considered for large- and small-scale CBI efforts. Table 3.1 shows the 10 steps.

The emphasis of this book is on the psychology of CBI design. Those steps in the CBI design process which are common to design

TABLE 3.1 Steps in CBI Design, Production, and Testing

Step 1. Conduct environmental analysis
- Proposed use of courseware
- Available hardware
- User attitudes

Step 2. Conduct knowledge engineering
- Course content
- Concept/task analysis

Step 3. Establish instructional goals and objectives
- Instructional goals
- Specific objectives and student performance levels
- Instructional objective taxonomies

Step 4. Sequence topics and tasks in CBI lessons (this is the main topic of Chapter 5)

Step 5. Write courseware
- Introductions, interactions, remedial sequences, review, and tests (this is the main topic of Chapter 6).
- Tailor interactions for specific student performance levels (this is the main topic of Chapter 7).

Step 6. Design each frame, the student–computer dialogue, and the student performance record (this is the main topic of Chapter 4)

Step 7. Program the computer
- Programming languages
- Authoring languages and packages

Step 8. Produce accompanying documents

Step 9. Evaluate and revise the CBI (this is the main topic of Chapter 8)

Step 10. Implement and follow-up as necessary

of instruction in any medium, as well as steps not so closely related to the psychology of design, are described in this chapter. Information about environmental analysis, knowledge engineering, establishing goals and objectives, programming, documentation, and revision/implementation is presented in this chapter. Steps more directly related to the psychology of CBI design are discussed in later chapters. Chapters 4 through 8, respectively, discuss the steps related to frame design, topic sequencing, frame writing, writing instruction for specific performance levels, and evaluation.

Step 1. Conduct Environmental Analysis

An environmental analysis (sometimes called *front-end analysis*) makes clear the context in which the courseware will be used. In some cases, environmental analysis is straightforward, for example, when a designer is asked to provide a reinforced drill or game to accompany a specific chapter in a textbook, or to serve as free-time activity for students. In those cases, the context in which the courseware will be used is fairly clear. However, much of the time, particularly where CBI is being used in new situations, the customer or potential user may not have available details about the context of the CBI, and the designer will need to uncover the information. In many cases, an environmental analysis must be conducted at the location where CBI is to occur.

An environmental analysis is no trivial thing—failing to conduct an environmental analysis can result in courseware that will not be used, no matter how sound the instructional sequences or how colorful the graphics. Many CBI designers have experienced this unfortunate and costly situation. Developing sound courseware that nobody wants is not just a waste of time and money, it can also damage a CBI designer's reputation, although not as much as developing unsound and useless courseware. Project managers should make sure that courseware is not developed in a vacuum.

Proposed Use of Courseware

When conducting an environmental analysis, the CBI designer must determine if the courseware is to replace an existing course or function as a completely new course. In addition, it must be determined if the courseware is to be used as primary instruction, is to serve as additional practice with material already introduced by other means, or used as adjunctive instruction. A determination about the number of separate courseware programs needed should be made.

Also important is the stability of the proposed course content—is the material constant from term to term, or will frequent updates be required? Some courseware programs are easy to change, but others are not. For example, a videodisk player, which projects full-color, high-resolution *(high-fidelity)* graphics and still and moving pictures, may be used to several important advantages when incorporated into CBI. The disadvantage is that a videodisk, once manufactured, cannot be modified, as of this writing, without time and expense. An environmental analysis must weigh the issues of required fidelity versus flexibility in courseware: high fidelity is often less flexible. Therefore, high fidelity in courseware should be designed only for stable course content. A related issue concerns the number of students who will use the courseware and the frequency of courseware use. As these numbers increase, courseware flexibility may decrease, but so should courseware durability. That is, the content should be applicable even if small changes in course content should occur.

In some settings, classroom layout can cause potential problems for courseware use. In many locales, computers are displaced from classrooms and relegated to the computer center, a place where many students do not wish to go, perhaps because it is distant from classrooms, or because it is a somber place where talking ("Only one student per terminal allowed"), eating, and drinking are not allowed. How many of us would rather do our homework in a computer center as opposed to our rooms at home? In such circumstances, the CBI designer might recommend decentralization of computer resources or suggest how the instructor might best set up contingencies to ensure student use of the courseware in a computer center, or program plentiful reinforcers in the courseware when it appears that students may be reluctant to use the courseware.

Available Hardware

The environmental analysis assesses the computers on which the courseware will be run and suggests the courseware complexity that is possible at the locale. Is the courseware to be run on a mainframe computer, personal computer with extended memory, or a smaller computer? Other concerns are the number of computers, amount of memory, and printers available. In some cases, the courseware designer might be asked to recommend hardware. Thus it behooves CBI designers to learn as much as they can about hardware for CBI.

User Attitudes

Once the decision is made by administrators to purchase CBI, the users of greatest concern are instructors and students. Even though computers are today ubiquitous, their popularity has been achieved relatively recently, and thus attitudes toward use of computers vary widely. One day consumers are hyped that small children without computer literacy are doomed to unimportant lots in life, and the next day a backlash suggests that only people involved in complicated business need buy computers. Many educators and students enjoy CBI, but many do not. It is wise to allow the dissenters their voice.

A recent personal experience of the author illustrates the point. While conducting an environmental analysis, the author told a student that she was assessing the possibility of incorporating CBI into a future version of the course, and the student volunteered that he owned a home computer. Next he was asked how CBI might have helped in his present studies. The student said that he would not like to participate in CBI, and furthermore, that he would not want his children subjected to it. When asked why, he replied that human interaction (taken to mean conversation with a caring instructor) was critical in learning. Later, this view was articulated by other students and instructors. This viewpoint, that CBI depersonalizes instruction, is common; obviously, all of us want the support of a good human instructor.

If the environmental analysis reveals negative attitudes, what does the CBI designer do about it? One, the CBI designer may provide information that CBI should not replace all contact with instructors and other students. Two, the CBI designer might point out that students in CBI lessons may make errors, and in some cases, ask questions of the computer, without embarrassment. In these respects, CBI is personal. Courseware programs should be patient and kind and employ no negative contingencies. Third, if negative opinions appear to threaten the success of a CBI program, a more formal educational approach, preferably using CBI, might be developed to inform consumers and change attitudes before courseware is tested or implemented. In the case of the student mentioned above, assurances that the CBI was not going to replace human teachers occasioned a response of "Oh well, in THAT case. . . . "

Step 2. Conduct Knowledge Engineering

Knowledge engineering describes the process used by a CBI designer to collect material (knowledge) related to the content of the proposed courseware and to organize (engineer) it into a course. At this step of courseware design, a statement of the general objectives of the course is produced. To initiate this activity, the CBI designer schedules interviews with subject matter or course-content experts or instructors experienced with the course.

Understanding Course Content

A subject-matter expert is a person who has mastered the content to be taught. A subject-matter expert is someone working in any field, for example government, science, art, social service, or industry, who in all likelihood has little or no formal training in instructional design and/or computer technology. If asked to teach, many subject-matter experts would probably teach in the same way they were taught. Often this means that they would lecture, or advise students to read up on the topic and figure things out alone. A subject-matter expert might also be an educator who has mastered a body of knowledge and teaches it, but who is relatively unskilled in computer technology.

A CBI designer has expertise in topics such as those included in this book. Many CBI designers are also knowledgeable about computer technology (e.g., available hardware) and programming languages or authoring systems. Depending on their seniority or availability of resources, CBI designers enlist computer programmers to write the computer code for their programs, although many designers program their own lessons.

Subject-matter experts and CBI designers frequently come together to design CBI. A subject-matter expert might decide to develop a CBI lesson, but might not have instructional design (especially CBI design) or computer technology expertise, and thus would seek out an instructional designer. The reverse situation often happens: instructional designers are asked by a customer to develop a CBI lesson about topics in which the designer has little or no knowledge. The instructional designer then seeks out a subject-matter expert. Some subject-matter experts develop CBI using simple authoring packages (designed for quick and easy production of a CBI lesson), and some CBI designers develop CBI for those topics (usually elementary CBI or instructional games) that they have mastered. However, CBI designers and subject-matter experts collaborate very frequently as the demand for CBI increases in hundreds of applications.

Conduct Concept (Topic) or Task Analysis

In addition to collecting course content, knowledge engineering includes concept and task analysis. A *concept* analysis (also called topic analysis) generates a list of topics and subtopics included in the course, often presented in outline or tree diagram form. A *task* analysis generates a list of the steps and substeps involved in a procedure. A topic or task analysis organizes course content and clarifies the relation of one topic to another. The topic or task analysis is preliminary to stating instructional objectives and producing the sequence of topics, subtopics, steps, and substeps that will be used in the courseware.

Knowledge Engineering for Intelligent CBI

In addition to the process of extracting course content from experts and other sources, knowledge engineering for intelligent CBI involves an additional activity. The knowledge bases (e.g., the course content, teaching strategy, and student file) have to be formatted. This generally requires programming expertise, so either the CBI designer or programmer accomplishes this step in knowledge engineering.

Step 3. Establish Goals and Instructional Objectives

Stating Goals

Establishing goals and objectives for instruction is a critical step in the design of instruction. Without objectives, instruction has no purpose. As obvious a statement as this is, teachers or course designers frequently do not clearly state the goals of instruction before they begin to teach. You may recall from Chapter 2 that Skinner (1984, p. 950) writes that "be[ing] clear about what is to be taught" is one of the most important ways in which we can improve instruction.

We derive objectives from general goals, specified on a number of levels: societal, educational systems, schools, and courses. Goals are statements about what instruction should accomplish. Goals suggest objectives which are detailed statements about the learning that should be accomplished.

Educational system goals are based on society's expectations of what schools as an institution should accomplish. Educational system goals might include something like "develop knowledgeable citizens" or "train productive employees." Schools are set up to accomplish the mission of the system. School goals might include such things as "develop student intellectual capabilities" and "improve student physical conditioning." Schools set up courses to accomplish these goals. The goal of the course is to accomplish a school goal. An example of a course goal might be "to teach concepts and applications in the area of eighth-grade American history."

A course designer may find it helpful to state goals for several levels, depending on the novelty or complexity of the educational setting. A CBI designer writing courseware for purposes that are clearly specified may need only to specify a course (or even lesson) goal. A CBI designer writing courseware for several related courses within a new curriculum or school may need to specify general goals from the system to the lesson. If designing courseware for foreign countries, a designer should generally understand the social goals for education in that country.

A goal statement includes four components:

- A general statement of the subject matter.
- The purpose of the course (e.g., critical, optional, free time, background for other courses).
- The proportion of topics to tasks included (e.g., intellectual material, performance tasks).
- An estimate of the performance level required for each topic (e.g., acquisition, fluency building, generalization, mastery maintenance).

Goals need not be strictly formatted, but the samples below illustrate goals that might be written for three different courseware applications.

Example 1.

"The courseware for this tenth-grade math class is designed to introduce and provide practice in teaching the differences between direct and inverse proportion. This topic is covered in the regular textbook, but in the past, the instructor has found that these topics are difficult for students to grasp in the early stages. Mastery of these topics (or concepts) is critical to success in this tenth-grade course. Students will be introduced briefly to the topic by their teacher and be asked to complete the CBI lesson. The textbook lesson will remain required, but the teacher feels that more practice is needed than that required by the textbook lesson. Students should learn the definitions of direct and inverse proportion, be able to determine from a graph if two functions are directly or inversely related, and state if two functions, picked from the student's own experience, are inversely or directly related."

Example 2.

"The goal of this course is to provide application and generalization practice in teaching helicopter pilots to drop life-lines on target. The students are all licensed pilots. Because of the expense involved in conducting real-life life-line drops, the organization would like their pilots to be able to practice this task in a computer training simulation. Students will be tested several times on the simulation, and then in field exercises. Successful completion of the simulated drops is prerequisite to the field test, which is an annual requirement for licensure. The ultimate test, of course, will be student performance in a situation which nature, not instructors, will set up. Therefore, the students must be highly prepared."

Example 3.

"This courseware is designed to be an instructional game for teaching the kings and queens of England. This courseware will be free-time activity. Topic mastery as taught by the student's textbook is required, but students will not be assigned to participate in the instructional game. It is expected, however, that students who use this game as free-time activity will acquire fuller and longer-lasting mastery of the kings and queens of England than students who do not use the game."

Writing Specific Objectives

Specific instructional objectives develop from goals. Clearly stated instructional objectives are requisite to the design of instruction.

The purpose of a specific objective is to describe precisely what the student will be able to do after completing a segment, lesson, or unit of instruction. Using the specific objectives, we write text, interactions, and test items. A specific objective includes (1) the conditions under which the student will perform, (2) the action required, (3) how the student will demonstrate the action, and (4) the mastery level required.

First, the conditions under which the student will perform are stated. Conditions specify the antecedent stimuli. These conditions will be set up for the student following a unit, lesson, or segment of instruction.

Second, the objective specifies exactly, with a verb and an object, what action the student is to perform. The verb used should be an action verb. For example, the student will *point to*, or *write*, or *list*, or *match*. Verbs that do not denote action, such as *understand*, *appreciate*, or *develop a feeling for*, are not used in specific instructional objectives. Selection of a verb to use in a specific instructional objective is important and is discussed more thoroughly in the next section. The object of the action verb specifies the task. For example, the student will list the colors of the spectrum. The verb is *list*, the object is *colors of the spectrum*. The action verb, of course, must be something the student can do on the computer.

Third, the objective specifies how the student will demonstrate the skill. In other words, the action required of the student in practice interactions or tests is specified. For example, the student will list the colors of the spectrum by typing in a series of color names.

Fourth, the objective states the mastery level required and the criterion for acceptable performance. This criterion might be called the *standard*. Examples of standards might include: acquisition level, a minimum of 60 percent correct; mastery level, 5 correct answers in 5 minutes; generalization level, 10 correct answers in 20 minutes with no more than two errors. A CBI designer must determine with the help of the instructor or subject-matter expert the criteria corresponding to the desired performance levels. For example, is 5 correct in 5 minutes acquisition or mastery? It depends on the course content.

The list below includes sample objectives that might be accomplished with CBI.

- Following completion of the lesson on probability, given 10 correct and 5 incorrect definitions, the student will identify correct definitions of probability by pointing to 6 of the 10 correct definitions in 10 minutes (acquisition level).
- Following the unit on world rivers, given 25 world river names, the student will type in the name of the country in which the river originates, to mastery level, to an accuracy of 5 correct names in 1 minute.
- Following the lesson on generating new solutions, given a computer screen and light pen, the student will trace the lion through the maze, to generalization level, three different ways in 20 minutes, without crossing a solid line.

In some cases, CBI customers require detailed specification of specific instructional objectives and an explanation of how each instructional interaction and test item relates to each objective. Designers must be able to demonstrate these relations.

Instructional Objective Taxonomies

Sometimes it is difficult to translate goals into specific instructional objectives. For one thing, it may be difficult to ensure that the specific objectives chosen adequately cover the content. Instructional objective taxonomies cue a designer to consider all important aspects of a topic.

Three taxonomies are presented in this chapter. The first taxonomy concerns broad classes of learning objectives. The second covers objectives related to verbal learning. The third taxonomy covers objectives related to teaching physical tasks.

Briggs & Wager (1981), Gagne (1977), and Gagne and Briggs (1979) present a classification of five broad classes of learning objectives. The taxonomy includes sample action verbs which are useful for writing objectives for each of the five classes. The five classes and sample associated verbs (from Briggs & Wager, 1981) include:

- Verbal information learning (verbs: *list, recite, state, summarize*).
- Intellectual skills (verbs: *discriminate, identify, classify, demonstrate, generate*).
- Cognitive strategies (verb: *originate*).
- Motor skills (verb: *execute*).
- Attitudes (verb: *choose*).

Verbal information learning refers to rote learning, learning of facts, and summarizing information. Intellectual skills include discriminating, using concepts, using rules, and problem solving. Cognitive strategies include new ways of organizing and explaining. Motor skills are physical movements. Attitudes refer to dispositions or beliefs held about something. Using this taxonomy, an instructional designer develops objectives that cover the subject matter of the course, lesson, or segment using as many categories as necessary.

Another taxonomy provides a more in-depth perspective on verbal, intellectual, and cognitive skills. A taxonomy of verbal behavior includes verbal information, intellectual skills, and cognitive strategies. This taxonomy covers verbal behavior and is useful in selecting instructional objectives (Chase, 1985; Johnson & Chase, 1981). Verbal behavior includes everything a person says, writes, and thinks. The taxonomy considers the major classes of verbal behavior described by Skinner (1957) and applies them to instructional objectives. The taxonomy is presented in Table 3.2.

Take as an example the general goal: "This is a CBI module in educational psychology. The purpose of the module is to provide application practice in distinguishing positive from negative reinforcement. Generalization skills are required." This goal involves verbal behavior. The following list, developed from the verbal behavior objective taxonomy, includes specific objectives that relate to that goal.

- Given a list of psychological terms and definitions, the student will match term to definition, 5 correct in 1 minute with no errors.
- Given a definition of either positive or negative reinforcement, the student will correctly label the definition, 5 correct in 1 minute with no errors.
- Given the term positive reinforcement, the student will type the correct definition within 2 minutes.
- Given a scenario, the student will correctly label the scenario as one depicting either positive or negative reinforcement within 5 minutes.
- Given a scenario, the student will correctly present a positive reinforcer into the scenario within 5 minutes.

To select objectives from the list above, the designer determines if the student is to match (correct definition to the term), recognize

**TABLE 3.2 Verbal Skills Instructional Taxonomy
(Adapted from Chase, 1985; Johnson & Chase, 1981)**

Objective: Say something exactly as it was said
Task Type: Copy aloud after hearing it
Example: Correctly repeat the following lines from *Hamlet*. Copy my intonation.

Objective: Say something exactly as it was written
Task Type: Copy aloud after reading it
Example: Please read and pronounce correctly the following medical terms.

Objective: Write something exactly as it was written
Task Type: Copy in writing from written word
Example: Correctly copy the following Chinese characters.

Objective: Write something exactly as it was said
Task Type: Dictation; copy in writing after hearing it
Example: Correctly spell the following terms for the lab equipment as I say them.

Objective: Ask for assistance
Task Type: Request help
Example: At some point, you will not be able to proceed without asking for help. Your job is to ask the right question so that you can complete the project.

Objective: Define general rules of general features that define a term, topic, or concept, without access to the rules or features
Task Type: Give definition from memory
Example: Define reinforcement without looking at your notes. Compare and contrast discriminative and establishing stimuli.

Objective: Identify descriptions of specific instances of a topic or phenomenon
Task Type: Example identification; select definition
Example: Say which of the following scenarios is an example of positive reinforcement.

Objective: State original examples of a phenomenon
Task Type: Exemplification
Example: Give an original example of reinforcement. Write an original poem using iambic pentameter.

Objective: Describe the specific characteristics of environmental events as they occur
Task Type: Example component
Example: Identify at least three distinctive features of each of the wines in the goblets in front of you.

Objective: Specify a term or label that can be used to categorize a group of environmental events
Task Type: Example identification
Example: Say whether each of the following videotape scenarios illustrates assertive or aggressive behavior.

Objective: Combine any two or more of the tasks above
Task Type: Combination
Example: Describe what general principle is referred to on page x, and give an example of this principle from your experience.

(label the definition), recall (write the definition), or apply the knowledge (perhaps in scenarios). Determining the range of possible objectives can be very time consuming.

Objectives for physical tasks or procedures may be developed along the same general lines. Table 3.3 provides a sample taxonomy of objectives for teaching procedures.

Using one of these taxonomies, which cover the range of potential objectives, will help a designer determine that the scope of selected instructional objectives is adequate. The objectives should be stated clearly and precisely and should cover everything to be learned in a lesson or segment. Good courseware spells out its objectives, either on the screen or in accompanying documentation. If objectives in commercial software are not spelled out, the teacher will have to review the courseware and determine what objectives would be met by using it.

Step 4. Sequence Topics and Tasks

The overview sequence tells the order in which topics, subtopics, tasks, and subtasks will be taught. Any of a number of sequence plans, discussed in Chapter 5, may be selected.

Step 5. Write Courseware

The CBI course consists of several types of frames: introductions, interactions, remedial, review, and tests. Many designers first write test items for each instructional objective, then write practice interactions for each test item, then write remedial sequences for each interaction, and finally, write introductions and review frames.

TABLE 3.3 Instructional Taxonomy for a Procedural Task

Objective:	Copy the procedure
Example:	Type *asdf* with your left hand, exactly as I have shown you
Objective:	Perform parts of the procedure without assistance
Example:	We have been through the steps in converting decimal to hexadecimal numbers. In hexadecimal, how old is a 34-year-old person? The first number is 1; what is the second number?
Objective:	Perform the procedure in response to a problem context where the procedure is required
Example:	The oil filter needs to be changed; please change it.
Objective:	Perform the procedure when suggestions for performing it are not given
Example:	Student presented with a copy machine making poor copies and asked to fix it.

Writing frames in this order helps assure that the instructional objectives are taught and tested, and helps keep down the number of frames used. (The reader should note the importance of good instructional objectives; they serve as a basis for a course.) Writing these elements is described in Chapter 6.

Interactions are tailored to specific student performance levels. Chapter 7 describes how to tailor interactions for each level: acquisition, fluency building, generalization, and mastery maintenance.

On a practical level, how does the CBI designer transmit the course plan to the computer programmer? One approach to the graphical layout of course plans is offered by Stephens (1985). Figure 3.1 shows the general notation used to diagram a lesson, topic within the lesson, and subtopic. This approach is a helpful first step in conveying lesson flow to the programmer.

At the subtopic level, even greater detail may be required in a graphic layout. Table 3.4 presents a sample of how introductions, interactions, remedial sequences, reviews, and tests may be scheduled within a topic. Seasoned designer/programmers can produce courseware using such a graphic.

In many cases, the designer is asked to specify on paper a more detailed design than that pictured in the preceding figures. One way of conveying this more detailed information is called *storyboarding*. A storyboard is one page used to illustrate one frame. One storyboard includes the words and graphics to be presented on the frame and directions about what frames follow depending on student responses. Hundreds of frames may be involved even in short lessons. A sample storyboard is presented in Figure 3.2. Storyboarding, a time-consuming process, is inevitable for those designers who do not write their own computer code and must convey the course plan to a programmer, or for those whose customers wish to review a detailed document before programming begins. As the designer–programmer team becomes more experienced, it develops shortcuts to storyboarding. Potential shortcuts in this process include: programming your own material, using a word processor to create storyboards, and developing an association with a programmer who can read your shorthand.

Step 6. Design Each Frame

Frame design refers to the layout of elements within a frame and concerns consistency, type size, colors, graphics, and clarity.

LESSON OUTLINE

TOPIC OUTLINE

SUBTOPIC OUTLINE

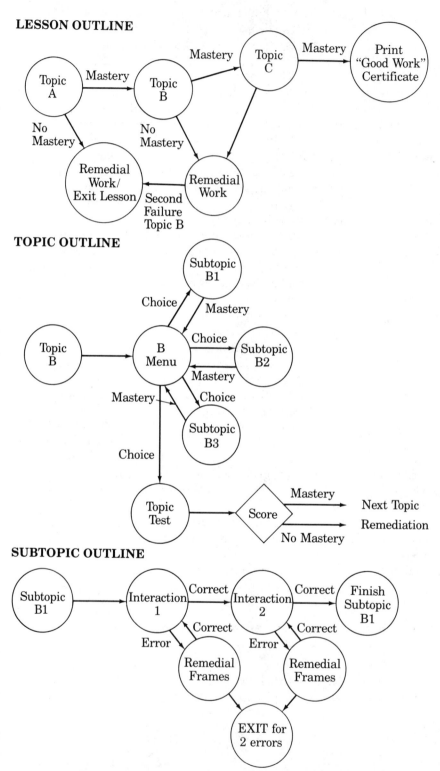

Figure 3.1. Schematic for a lesson, topic, and subtopic (following Stephens, 1985).

TABLE 3.4 Detailed Courseware Plan

Topic X

    Introduction to Topic X

    Subtopic 1

Introduction to subtopic 1	
Interaction: Identify A	Remedial frames
Interaction: Identify A	Remedial frames
Interaction: Define A	Remedial frames
Review of subtopic 1	
Test of subtopic 1	Contingent branch

    Subtopic 2

Introduction to subtopic 2	
Interaction: Define A	Remedial frames
Interaction: Identify B	Remedial frames
Interaction: Define B	Remedial frames
Review of subtopic 2	
Test of subtopic 2	Contingent branch

    Subtopic 3

Introduction to subtopic 3	
Interaction: Apply A	Remedial frames
Interaction: Apply B	Remedial frames
Review of subtopic 3	
Test of subtopic 3	Contingent branch

    Topic X Test

        Review of subtopics 1, 2, and 3

        Test of subtopics 1, 2, and 3

        Present total score and prescription

    Repeat for each topic in the lesson

These elements interact with the designer's plan for instructional frames. Frame layout and well-designed instruction can either enhance or ruin the other in CBI. This topic is discussed in Chapter 4. This topic was discussed ahead of steps subsequent to it in the 10-step process so that the reader would understand how frames are designed and be able to make good use of the frames provided as illustrations in subsequent chapters.

Step 7. Program the Computer

Understanding programming languages is an important concern of a CBI designer. As mentioned previously, the CBI designer frequently interacts with programmers, and in some cases, bears the

```
                    ┌─────────────────────────────────┐
                    │  FRAME 26    TITLE: _____ │
Enter Text:         │                                 │
                    │                                 │
Enter Question:     │                                 │
                    │                                 │
Answer Space:       │                                 │
                    │                                 │
Feedback:           │   ───────────────────────────── │
                    │  HELP    MAIN MENU    BACK   NEXT│
                    └─────────────────────────────────┘
```

Correct Answer(s): _____
Feedback if Correct: _____
If Correct, go to Frame # _____

Incorrect Answer(s): _____
Feedback for first error: _____ Go to Frame # _____
Feedback for second error: _____ Go to Frame # _____
Feedback for third error: _____ Go to Frame # _____

Figure 3.2. Sample storyboard for simple branching CBI lesson.

programming responsibility. In addition, CBI designers bring their expertise in learning theory when evaluating and using authoring languages.

Distinctions may be made among three techniques of course programming: general programming languages, authoring languages, and frame-based authoring packages. These are described below.

General Programming Languages

General programming languages require the programmer to enter lines of computer code to construct the course. The first word of the lines is often a verb or "command." Examples of programming languages that are often used to write CBI include BASIC, FOR-TRAN, COBOL, C, and APL. LISP and PROLOG are the languages most used to write intelligent CBI. These languages are general-purpose programming languages, used for more purposes than authoring courseware. Below is a sample of 22 lines of BASIC programming, taken from a longer program by Orwig (1983, p. 102):

```
1080   PRINT "IN WHAT YEAR DID FLORIDA BECOME A
       STATE?"
1090   PRINT "        1.   1840
1100   PRINT "        2.   1845
1110   PRINT "        3.   1861
1120   PRINT "        4.   1868
1130   PRINT
1140   GET SA$
1150   C$ = "2"
1160   RETURN
2000   REM   JUDGE ANSWER
2010   SC = 2
2020   IF SA$ = C$ THEN SC = 1
2030   RETURN
3000   REM   REWARDS
3010   PRINT
3020   ON R GOTO 3040,3060,3080,3100,3120
3030   REM   REWARDS
3040   PRINT "GREAT!"
3060   PRINT "SUPER"
3080   PRINT "FANTASTIC"
3100   PRINT "YOU'RE REALLY GOING NOW"
3120   PRINT "THAT'S GREAT"
```

This sample comes from a program that provides any of five reward messages if the student correctly selects 1845 as the year Florida became a state.

The following line from a LISP program instructs the computer to sort practice problems, in order from the least to the most complicated.

(sort fact-list #´ (lambda (a b) (< (num-deps a) (num-deps b))))

Authoring Languages

Authoring languages also require the programmer to enter lines of computer code, but the languages are used only for writing courseware. PILOT and PLANIT (Frye, 1980) are programming languages used only for writing courseware. These languages are commercially available and may be used on a variety of computers. Some CBI systems, such as PLATO, TICCIT, and IBM, which use special computers also have their own courseware authoring languages. TUTOR is the PLATO authoring language.

To illustrate the use of a courseware-authoring language, PILOT will be used as an example. The PILOT language has two modes: author and student. Courseware is written and revised in author mode, and run in student mode. Using a computer that has two disk drives, the authoring program, on a *system* disk (which must be purchased), is used in one drive, and a blank diskette that becomes the lesson disk is used in the other drive. As the programmer programs, the courseware is written to the lesson disk. The student mode is run using the system disk in one disk drive and the lesson disk in the other disk drive.

A PILOT programmer can use any of six types of instructions: text, response, control, computation, special effects, and file handling. Text instructions create the information and questions presented to the student, response instructions set the computer to accept and judge student responses, and these types of instructions are most frequently used.

In PILOT author mode, four editors are available: to create text, graphics, special characters, and sound effects. As an example, the author may select the text editor from a menu of choices containing the four editors. If the text editor is selected, another menu appears containing the choices: create a new lesson, edit an existing lesson, run the lesson, print, delete, and quit. For each of those choices, still another menu is presented; for example, if edit is selected, the next choices are copy, delete, find, insert, jump, repeat, exchange, and quit. When one of those is chosen, the package again prompts. For example, if you chose to delete, the package will ask you what to delete.

Using PILOT, however, is not a matter of simply filling in the blanks; ultimately, an instruction (one of the 26) must be entered as the first word on the left of a line of computer code, and the information entered on the right of the line. For example, to tell the computer to deliver feedback for a correct answer, the programmer might enter on one line

    TY   Correct!

and for an incorrect answer the programmer might enter

    TN   Sorry, try again. What is 2 + 3(53)?

Below is a simple example of how PILOT is used to judge an exact match answer.

    T   This is the lesson.   (Text)

T	What color is a fire truck?	(Text question)
A		(Student answer)
M	Red	(Answer exact match)
TY	You are correct	(Text if correct)
TN	No, fire trucks are red!	(Text if incorrect)

There are no restrictions on what you place in any PILOT frame. Unlike general-purpose languages, such as BASIC, COBOL, and FORTRAN, however, PILOT prompts a programmer to build courses.

Frame-Based Authoring Packages

In contrast to the freehand constructions allowed by languages are frame-based authoring packages. A frame-based authoring package prompts the designer or programmer to enter the exact information for each frame. The programmer or designer enters no, or very little, computer code. These packages make programming easy, following training in their use. (Some packages are more difficult to use than others, due to their designs. In addition, the more capabilities they have, the more there is to learn.) There are numerous authoring packages available, ranging in price and capability. Frame-based authoring packages typically contain author and student modes. Like some courseware authoring languages, they also prompt the programmer. Authoring packages, however, allow the programmer to fill in blanks instead of writing actual lines of computer code. Knowledge of computer programming commands is unnecessary.

In author mode, a package may prompt the programmer to enter text frames, then a query frame, then a feedback frame. A very simple example of authoring package prompts follows:

Enter the text you want the student to see on this frame:
Enter the question you want the student to answer:
What is the right answer:
What feedback do you want if the student is correct:
    If correct, branch to which frame:
What feedback do you want if the student is incorrect:
    If incorrect, branch to which frame:
Name of this frame:
Enter the text you want the student to see on this frame:
etc.

There are several authoring packages that provide both a fill-in-the-blank capability as well as a command-driven authoring language. These packages assume that when a beginner-level author becomes more skilled, he or she will graduate to the command language level that is more difficult to use, but provides more capability.

Evaluating Programming Languages, Authoring Languages, and Packages

In general, programming and authoring languages offer flexibility, but time and practice are required to become fluent in them. In many cases, the capabilities offered by programming and authoring languages far outweigh the costs. On the other hand, many packages are simple to learn compared to languages, although both require training. Although courses authored with packages may not be as versatile as courses authored with languages, ease of use may be an important factor, especially if the designer is to create the course without the help of a programmer. Neither language nor package is better; the selection of a language or package depends on the resources available (including time, money, available hardware, software, and programming expertise) and the intended use (such as formal or informal use, limited or widespread use).

Each coursewriter selects an authoring system (whether it be a language or package) depending on the circumstances. For example, the TUTOR authoring language must be used for writing courses for the PLATO system. An inexpensive test-authoring package might be chosen to generate practice and test items for use on the classroom microcomputer.

A language or package with free or at least flexible sales arrangements should be chosen to author courseware for sale on the open market. Courses developed with some packages can be used only by the purchaser of the authoring package unless financial arrangements are made with the package publisher. Restricted rights systems are more suited to those who develop courses to be used on specific computers for their own limited uses. Publishers of the various languages and packages will usually negotiate an agreement with a coursewriter who wants to mass produce a course.

Regardless of the system chosen, outlining the characteristics of authoring systems may help in the evaluation and selection process. Table 3.5 presents some criteria that are important in evaluating and authoring system.

Perhaps the key criteria for evaluating authoring systems concern the types of information allowed per frame, and the responsivity available in answer judging (Cook, 1983, 1984). Some systems limit the type of information that can be programmed into any one

TABLE 3.5   Evaluating Authoring Systems

AUTHORING SYSTEM ALLOWS YOU TO:

Yes   No

____ ____ Present text
____ ____ Present questions
____ ____ Cue student response

Accept answers:
____ ____ Multiple-choice
____ ____ True-false
____ ____ Matching
____ ____ Constructed responses such as fill-in-the-blanks or short-answer

Specify correct answers:
____ ____ Exact matches only are accepted as correct
____ ____ Accept misspellings as correct
____ ____ Accept synonyms as correct
____ ____ Accept a long answer as correct based on the presence of critical words somewhere in the student response

Specify incorrect answers:
____ ____ Only anticipated wrong responses accepted as incorrect
____ ____ Unanticipated wrong responses accepted as errors

Implement other desirable features:
____ ____ Program a HELP feature
____ ____ Place a time limit on student responses
____ ____ Program branches sensitive to a variety of correct and incorrect responses
____ ____ Freely construct frame content (e.g., information, queries, and feedback may be presented in same frame)
____ ____ Keep records of student performance: time data, accuracy data, summaries available, variety of statistics available
____ ____ Use it easily
____ ____ Develop courseware within your budget
____ ____ Develop courseware on the hardware available
____ ____ Distribute or sell courses authored with the system, at what cost

frame—a frame must either present information, ask a question, or give feedback. This programming arrangement makes it difficult to implement the *critical response principle*, which states that "learning occurs when the learner makes an active response based upon critical features of the material [he or] she is supposed to learn about" (Cook, 1983, p. 1). If the stimulus material, the text, is not present when the learner responds, the learner's response will be impeded by memory demands; the learner will not even have had a chance to practice the new material in its earliest performance stage in the presence of the stimulus material. As performance improves, memory of the stimulus may become important, but in the early stages of acquisition and in the later stages of learning for more complex skills, the presence of the stimulus increases the likelihood of interaction.

Perhaps the second most critical criterion of authoring systems concerns the responsivity of the answer judging (or "parsing") capability of the system (Cook, 1984). Each system requires the programmer to program the student responses it accepts as correct and those it considers incorrect. A system that can handle only exact matches between student-entered and single, target responses is limited in its ability to shape an incorrect response into a correct one (Cook, 1984).

In a human teacher–student interaction, a good teacher quickly assesses an answer, gives praise for a correct (within limits) answer, offers encouragement for trying, or gives hints if answers are outside acceptable limits. Take an example of a teacher's question "What figure of speech uses the word 'is'? " If the correct answer is "metaphor," the CBI system should be able to accept as correct misspellings (or typographical errors) of the word "metaphor," and any misspelling of the word, with or without the words "the" or "a." A human teacher would probably accept mispronunciations and misspellings in a student's answer to the question. Some systems even make it easy to accept synonyms as correct answers.

As for errors, if a student enters the word "simile" in response to the question above, the system should be able to say something like "A simile uses the words 'like' or 'as,' not 'is.' Please try again." Some systems which lack responsivity make it difficult to accept as correct anything other than exact matches. Thus the situation might arise where a student who enters "a metafor" might receive the relatively unhelpful "No. Please try again." The shaping process is impeded by such limits placed by the authoring system.

Problems with Authoring Systems

For all their benefits, authoring systems have their detractors. In fact, Bork (1984, p. 95) writes:

> The development . . . of authoring systems has been an enormous waste of money. Perhaps at this point billions of dollars, which could have gone into useful development of materials, have been spent on developing authoring systems. Hardly anything of any consequence has been developed with any of the authoring systems or languages which have been created. (TUTOR was an exception, possibly because of the almost infinite amounts of money that Control Data [the corporation that developed TUTOR] was willing to spend.)

Bork's objection seems to stem from his observation that, at present, people are looking for ways to use modern hardware and thus quickly develop something to do with the hardware. What is developed may not be especially important. Bork (1984) hopes that in the future, high-quality courseware will be available, and people will then seek hardware because they want to use the courseware.

Bork (1984) further describes the use of authoring systems as "single-individual" approaches to producing CBI. Single individuals may either produce courseware using a general-purpose language or an authoring language. Bork notes that single-individual approaches are difficult to use. Little material has been produced using them, and the materials produced are often dull. According to Bork (1984), the difficulties stem from two sources. First, few teachers are good programmers, and general-purpose languages are difficult to use. Second, authoring systems restrict program possibilities and may not reflect good principles of instructional programming.

The Future of Authoring Languages

Eberts and Brock (1984) note that automatic programming may improve authoring systems of the future. Automatic programming would combine the simplicity of authoring packages with the flexibility of languages. A programmer could enter a simple command, and the software would write the corresponding lines of computer code. Automatic programming of common steps would be accomplished by the computer through simple commands. Eberts and Brock also note as lesson-writing techniques develop and become more commonly used, new courseware will be more easily produced from existing courseware.

One interesting new concept in course authoring is the "Instructional Design Environment," now under development by the U.S. Army Research Institute and the Xerox Palo Alto Research Center. This design environment allows complex courses with graphics and simulation to be created by CBI designers, without programming. Figure 3.3 presents one designer screen (a script card) for a lesson in teaching data types in LOTUS 1-2-3. The figure shows 10 frames, with four student interaction frames (on lines beginning "Entering"), and finally a quiz.

Bunderson (1981) addresses the use of technological aids in courseware production. Bunderson has categorized these aids based on a widely used format for instructional design, called ISD, for Instructional Systems Development (TRADOC, 1975). The steps in ISD include:

- Analysis of training need.
- Design of lessons and tests.
- Development of materials.
- Implementation of materials.
- Control of instruction, which includes field evaluation and revision.

Bunderson (1981) suggests four categories of technological aids to authoring which might make easier the implementation of the ISD model.

1. Author prompting systems, which lead the writer through each step in the ISD process.
2. Text and graphics editing systems, which allow revisions during materials development.
3. Formative evaluation systems, which assist in analysis and use of data gathered during implementation trials.
4. Author management systems, which track progress of design teams for administrative purposes.

Technological aids to courseware development are relatively new products, even relative to the recency of courseware. Bunderson (1981) notes that a promising direction would be development of an aid that would combine author prompting in the ISD steps and text/graphics editing. He writes that authoring systems presently available, for example TUTOR and IBM's Coursewriter, are programming languages and do not provide author prompts to the extent required.

In summary, many agree that available authoring systems are unwieldy, difficult to use, and lacking in pedagogical validity. While the goal of authoring systems—to provide quickly large amounts of high-quality courseware—is important, it appears that satisfactory authoring systems are not yet widely available. On the positive side, they allow for creation of new courseware, tailored to specific objectives, and they help fill the courseware void. In addition, they may be used by people who do not wish to write the enormous amount of computer code required to run a course.

Step 8. Produce Accompanying Documents

Documents such as handbooks or manuals accompanying courseware are written for students, instructors, and programmers. These

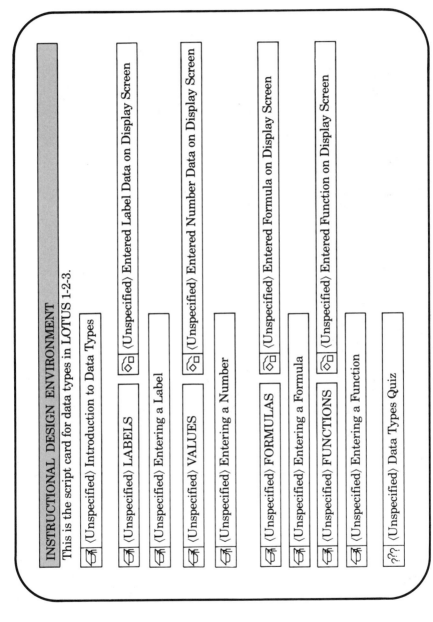

Figure 3.3. Designer's screen from "Instructional Design Environment" (courtesy of Joseph Psotka, Army Research Institute).

documents are written by CBI designers, CBI programmers, and professionals who specialize in document writing. All documents should be clearly written and include diagrams as necessary (Foehr & Cross, 1986).

The student handbook should contain step-by-step instructions on how to use the courseware. It should also contain an introduction to the course and course objectives. Figure 3.4 presents a clearly written student handbook page with introduction and course objectives. In some cases, the student may have to refer to the student handbook periodically throughout the course. If so, the integration of the handbook with the courseware must be clearly marked. The student should know how to get help when needed.

The instructor handbook should contain step-by-step instructions on how to use the computer and how to prepare the instructional site. Instructions for keeping records on student performance and interpreting student progress should be included.

Programmer's information is provided if on-site modifications to the courseware are possible. If included, programmer's information should contain an annotated copy of the computer code or frames. Instructions for modifying the program should be included.

Preparation of accompanying documents follows the same general process as preparing the CBI lesson itself:

Step 1: Determine the context in which the documents will be used.

Step 2: Determine what content needs to be included. Conduct task analyses of student, instructor, and programmer activities. Determine how many documents are needed.

Step 3: Establish objectives of each document.

Step 4: Determine order in which information will be presented.

Step 5: Write the information.

Step 6: Check the consistency of design on each page; include graphics as needed.

Step 7: Produce the document.

Step 8: Evaluate the document. Have a naive person follow your step-by-step instructions to see if he or she can successfully complete the activity using them. Have a colleague read the documents and point out unclear parts.

Step 9: Revise and distribute.

Step 10: Conduct follow-up assessments as needed.

KNOW YOUR MAN-MADE FIBERS

Know Your Man-Made Fibers is a practice computer program to educate individuals, especially youth, about man-made fibers. The program is designed for Apple IIe microcomputers and IBM PC microcomputers (and their compatibles).

Textile products in today's world often confuse individuals both young and old. Many people lack the necessary knowledge about textile fibers to make appropriate decisions in selecting apparel and home furnishings. The *Know Your Man-Made Fibers* computer program will aid people of all ages who want to learn more about textiles. The program focuses on the characteristics, uses and care of man-made fibers.

A dictionary of the terms used in the program appears as a part of the screen menu. To enhance learning, program participants should begin by experimenting with the dictionary and become familiar with the textile terms before using other parts of the program.

Accompanying the program is a pre- and post-test to evaluate the degree of learning (Appendix A). These instruments were used in the pilot testing of the computer program. The pre-test should be administered prior to the introduction of the study on man-made fibers. The post-test should be administered after the program is completed.

The computer program should be an integral part of the educational unit on man-made fibers. Evaluations from two pilot tests indicated the program would serve as a good tutorial method for students (junior high through college), as well as for volunteer leaders in Extension.

Objectives

After completing the *Know Your Man-Made Fibers* computer program, participants will be able to better:

- understand the characteristics of man-made fibers as they relate to everyday textile products.
- know the uses of certain man-made fibers as they relate to everyday textile products.
- apply appropriate care to man-made fiber textile products.
- interpret man-made fiber labeling.
- recognize the difference between generic and trademark labeling.

1

Figure 3.4. Page from student handbook accompanying CBI lesson "Know Your Man-Made Fibers." (courtesy of Nadine Hackler, University of Florida).

Step 9. Evaluate and Revise the CBI

CBI evaluation is discussed in Chapter 8. To preview, four types of courseware evaluations are desirable: structural evaluation of the form of the CBI, functional evaluation of the teaching-effectiveness of the CBI, evaluation of the cost-effectiveness of the CBI, and evaluation of user opinions of the CBI. These evaluations are best conducted at least twice in the cycle. The first courseware evaluation is conducted by CBI developers during development to assist them in improving the courseware before it is released. A second evaluation is conducted after release by potential users to determine the adequacy of the CBI for their purposes.

Before the courseware is released for the first time, an in-house review is conducted. The designer, programmer, and other consultants, as required, test the courseware. A typical user should also test the program. The smooth flow of the lesson, the correctness of the feedback given to both wrong and right answers, pleasant-looking frames with no typographical errors, and the ability of the program to provide assistance to the student if extra help is required are all important factors to evaluate. Areas of weakness are improved before the CBI is released.

Seldom are the cost- and training-effectiveness of CBI evaluated by those who produce or sell it; the task usually falls to potential users. Conducting such evaluations would no doubt benefit CBI designers, and evaluations by designers will probably become more frequent as the marketplace becomes more competitive. The goal of these evaluations is to determine if the courseware economically produces learning. (If potential users cannot take the time to test the courseware on students, they can evaluate the format or *structure* of the lesson and make inferences about teaching effectiveness.) Often, CBI is purchased first and tested later. In the case where large educational systems purchase first and test later, some instructors in the system may use the CBI and others will not. In the worst case of purchase first–test later, bad CBI is acquired and never used. Unfortunately, user opinions and information about teaching effectiveness rarely are fed back to CBI producers. Dellalana (1985) suggests that courseware publishers offer incentives for consumers to return student data to the publisher for analysis that will guide improvements for future versions.

CBI designers use evaluation results to change their courseware. Commercial publishers revise the courseware before it is released; instructors who produce their own courseware can revise their courseware as they see how their students perform using the courseware. Users should report back to CBI writers, and users should insist on only the highest-quality CBI. The topic of revision is covered in Chapter 8.

Step 10. Implement and Follow-Up

Implementation means delivering the courseware to the operational site, making sure that it runs on the available computer, and instructing personnel in its use. Designer assistance in implementation will help the users.

A CBI designer should follow-up his or her courseware to see if the users continue to be satisfied. Given that initial evaluations of functional effectiveness are rarely conducted, it should be no surprise that courseware follow-up is rare as well. However, consumers should be encouraged to report back to courseware producers to effect future needed revisions.

CBI Design–Production as a Collaborative Process

As mentioned earlier, some individuals produce useful CBI by themselves. A person who knows computer-based instruction design, the course content, and how to program can produce CBI, given the time and materials to do it. However, because many persons do not possess all three skills and because those who do seldom have the time and materials, much CBI design and production is a collaborative process.

The CBI designer–subject-matter expert collaborative process is outlined in Table 3.6. The CBI designer takes the initial lead. The CBI designer first conducts the environmental analysis to determine the context in which CBI will be used. During knowledge engineering, the CBI designer consults with the subject-matter expert. Because many subject-matter experts are unaccustomed to conducting concept and task analyses of their expertise, the CBI designer must ask probing questions to elucidate a general course analysis. The CBI designer also solicits copies of any existing material that would help in establishing instructional objectives and sequencing topics for instruction. CBI designer concerns also include the degree of

TABLE 3.6 Collaboration of CBI Designers with Subject-Matter Experts and Computer Programmers

Activity	People Involved
Step 1. Conduct environmental analysis	CBI designer
Step 2. Conduct knowledge engineering, collect course materials, topic/task analysis	CBI designer, subject-matter expert
Step 3. Establish goals and instructional objectives	CBI designer
Step 4. Sequence topics and tasks for instruction; secure approval of topics and sequences	CBI designer, subject-matter expert
Step 5. Write courseware	CBI designer
Step 6. Design each frame	CBI designer, programmer
Step 7. Program the computer	Programmer (or CBI designer)
Step 8. Produce accompanying document	CBI designer (or documentation specialist)
Step 9. Evaluate and revise the CBI	CBI designer, programmer, subject-matter expert
Step 10. Implement, secure user approval, follow up	CBI designer, programmer, subject-matter expert

topic difficulty and the relative importance of individual topics to the overall course. Difficult and important topics receive more emphasis in the course than simple, relatively unimportant topics.

While several informal contacts may occur in the interim, the next formal contact between CBI designer and subject-matter expert is held to obtain the expert's opinion on the reasonableness of the objectives and topic sequence suggested by the CBI designer. The subject-matter expert also approves the accuracy of the content, presented to the best of the CBI designer's understanding. Study questions, test questions, and practice exercises are discussed. Based on subject-matter expert input, adjustments to the proposed course outline may be made.

Next the CBI designer enriches the outline by adding introductions, reviews, and tests for each unit in the lesson, and by planning interactions and material presentation, response requirements, and feedback for each content point taught. These will be tested later by the subject-matter expert.

Hardware availability is assessed and a programming language is chosen, often through consultation with the programmer. The designer consults with a programmer concerning frame design. Next, the CBI designer writes computer code or generates the lesson using an authoring system, or arranges for this activity to be accomplished by a programmer. The formative courseware evaluations presented in Chapter 8 will be useful in guiding the CBI designer's work during this activity.

The CBI designer then delivers the package. A subject-matter expert or instructor tests it initially or tries it out on students. Regardless, the CBI designer should solicit critiques from instructors, subject-matter experts, and students.

The final step involves test and revision. In the best case, the CBI designer will have the opportunity to collect both student opinion and performance data, and revise the courseware as necessary. User approval is obtained, and the courseware is implemented.

Study Questions

Definition Questions

1. List the 10 steps in the CBI design, production, and evaluation process.
2. What information is important in an environmental analysis?
3. What is knowledge engineering? How does knowledge engineering contribute to the CBI design process?
4. What is a concept or task analysis?
5. How can instructional skills taxonomies help in defining specific instructional objectives?
6. What is meant by *frame design*?
7. What are two of the most important features of courseware authoring packages, according to Cook?
8. What are some important aspects in the design of CBI documentation?

Discussion Questions

1. Why is it important to conduct an environmental analysis prior to writing CBI?
2. Give an example of a CBI goal and several related specific instructional objectives. Check that your objectives contain all the needed information.
3. Select any concept and write one specific CBI objective for each level in the Chase instructional skills taxonomy.
4. Give an example of a procedure that could be taught using CBI.
5. What are the similarities and differences between courseware authoring languages and courseware authoring packages?
6. Practice evaluating some courseware authoring languages and packages if they are available.
7. Describe how CBI designers, subject-matter experts, and programmers collaborate to design, produce, and test CBI.

CHAPTER 4

Design of the Student–Computer Interface

The main topics of this chapter are:

- *Special characteristics of computer screens*
- *Student–frame interface*
- *Student–computer dialogue*
- *Design of student performance records*

Introduction

The term *student–computer interface* refers to the points of contact between the student and the computer. In this chapter, three such points of contact or interfaces are described: student–frame contact, student–computer dialogue, and student–performance record.

Student–frame interface design refers to the design of individual frames. The way a computer screen looks has important implications for a student's correct and efficient use of the material on the screen. A well-designed frame teaches properly, requires a minimal amount of time to interpret, and evokes positive student reactions. Designing computer screens is accomplished differently from designing textbook pages.

The *student–computer dialogue* refers to the way in which the student and computer talk with each other. The most common student–computer dialogue is the "menu," which allows the student to request something and the computer to respond by presenting the requested frames.

Student–performance record interface design refers to the design of the student's progress record. This record should provide accurate information in a clear manner and foster motivation.

Before these three topics are discussed, the special characteristics of computer screens will be described.

Special Characteristics of Computer Screens

People read about 25 percent faster from text pages than they do from computer displays (Gould, Alfaro, Barnes, Finn, Grischkowsky, & Minuto, 1987). These authors reported on a series of 10 experiments designed to isolate a single cause (e.g., computer experience, character size, type of font) of the slower reading speed. Gould et al. did not isolate a single cause, and the authors suggest that an interaction of factors accounts for the difference. The authors speculate that use of high-quality image and paperlike fonts will increase reading speed from a computer display.

CBI differs from other instructional media with respect to the way material can be displayed. Computer screens are shaped differently from textbook pages, and less information can be displayed at one time. A student must sit farther away from a computer screen than he or she does from a book and view the screen from a strict 90-degree angle. In addition, the glass on a computer screen can create glare. Finally, the resolution of images on computer screens is not sharp unless high-resolution graphics are used, and electronic print creates different visual stimuli than does print on paper. The design of a computer screen is therefore driven by a different set of circumstances than those which drive the content displayed on a textbook page. Display size, visual angle and distance, and physical properties of light all interact differently on a computer screen than they do with print on paper.

Several physical factors help students clearly view the monitor (Diffrient, Tilley, & Harman, 1981). Screen lighting should be brighter than the room lighting. This may be accomplished by increasing screen brightness or contrast or by reducing room brightness. Contrast should usually be kept very high and brightness adjusted (often reduced) as necessary. The eye must not be able to detect any flicker in the screen. The student should view the screen from a distance of about 16 inches. The distance from the chair seat upward to the computer should be from 14 to 35 inches. The student should view the screen at a 90-degree angle. The best acuity will be directly in front of the eyes. The screen should be located and designed for minimal head and eye movement.

Galitz (1981) summarized interviewees' responses concerning desirable characteristics of screens. These included:

• An orderly, clean, clutter-free appearance.

- An obvious indication of what is being shown and what should be done with it.
- Expected information where it should be.
- A clear indication of what relates to what.
- Plain simple English.
- A simple way of finding what is in the system and how to get it out.
- A clear indication of when an action could make a permanent change in the data or system operation.

Student–Frame Interface

Frame Functional Areas

Any frame must be carefully designed so that it conveys information clearly without being cluttered. One simple approach is to divide the screen into functional areas that remain consistent throughout the lesson (Heines, 1984). Screens may contain functional areas for:

- Orientation information such as screen title or frame number (e.g., "frame 45 of 64"). (This functional area is also present on textbook pages in the form of a page number and/or the chapter or section title.)
- Text (which may be new or review information).
- Graphics.
- Questions (interactions or test items, including directions for entering the response).
- Space for student responses.
- Space for feedback.
- Direction for advancing to next frame.
- Menu of options.

Heines (1984) suggests that area shape, location, and boundaries are important in determining functional areas on a screen. Non-overlapping blocks are good shapes for functional areas because they are consistent, straight, and usually easier than other shapes for a programmer to program. It is generally preferable to locate horizontal rather than vertical areas. We are accustomed to reading horizontally, and programming is often easier for horizontal than for vertical areas. Areas may be bounded with visible lines

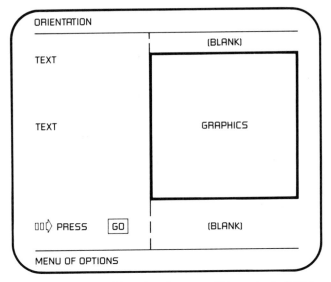

Figure 4.1. Sample layout of functional areas within a single frame (adapted from Heines, 1984, p. 23).

or with spacing. Figure 4.1 illustrates a sample placement of functional areas.

One useful test for good screen design is to glance at the screen and determine if all screen elements can be identified without reading the words on the screen (Galitz, 1981). To achieve screens that "pass the test," Galitz (1981, p.42) recommends, for a standard 24-line screen:

- Start each frame at the upper left-hand corner.
- Keep element locations constant.
- Place screen title in upper center, line 1.
- Place screen identifier number in upper right corner, line 1.
- Place menu options on the bottom line.
- Leave a blank line below the title line, and one line blank above the menu options line.
- Place the body of the screen between lines 3 and 22.
- Center the display; maintain balance or equal weighting between vertical halves of the display.

Figure 4.2 presents a sample frame that includes these elements.

Figure 4.3 presents a frame format used in a course in word processing. The sample that the student works on is presented in the "word-processing simulation area." Comments to the student

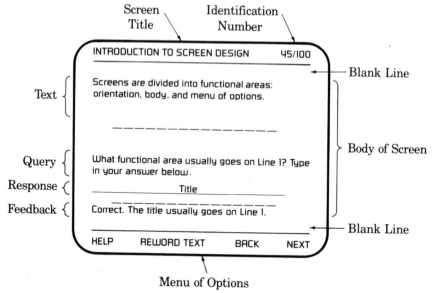

Figure 4.2. Sample screen with important screen elements.

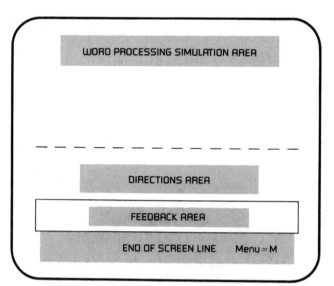

Figure 4.3. Screen format used in a lesson teaching word processing (courtesy of Training Section, U.S. Senate Computer Center).

are presented in the directions and feedback areas. The format is used throughout the course.

Single versus Multiple-Purpose Frames

Functional areas are identified on any frame, as mentioned above. This does not mean, however, that every area is used on every frame. Any single frame may serve a single or multiple purpose. However, any single frame should normally contain at least an orientation (title and identification number), a direction for advancing, and a menu of options, even if the frame has only one purpose.

A single-purpose frame is one that either presents information, asks a question, accepts an answer, or provides feedback. Thus a student must progress through several frames in order to complete a text plus interaction sequence. Arranging an interaction in this way is helpful in two instances. First, the material may be sufficiently detailed that presenting it all, plus an interaction, on a single frame would exceed the space constraints of a frame. Second, presenting an interaction separate from the text requires that the student remember information from previous screens. Thus, separating text and interaction can increase the difficulty of the interaction, a desirable circumstance in many instructional modules.

However, because interaction is so important in CBI, most frames should serve several purposes such as querying, accepting answers, and delivering feedback. A noted psychologist in the CBI field, Donald Cook (1984), makes the point that presenting a text frame that does not include an interaction fosters the notion that students are passive recipients of information.

The benefits of a multiple-purpose frame include:

- Text material is present when the student responds, thus reducing the chance of errors.
- The interactive nature of the computer–student relationship is highlighted; the student does not passively experience frames with no interaction.
- Feedback delivered next to the student response helps the student easily spot errors in answers.

In at least three instances, it appears critical that text and interaction be available on a single frame. First, early stages of learning are facilitated when there is no or very little time delay between presentation of text and responding; memory demands are decreased. Second, where text material is complicated, the student may be frustrated and make errors if important material is not

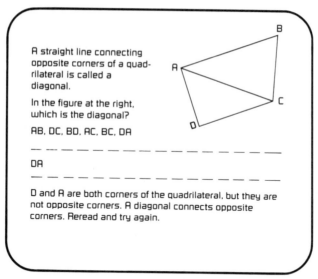

A straight line connecting
opposite corners of a quadrilateral is called a
diagonal.

In the figure at the right,
which is the diagonal?

AB, DC, BD, AC, BC, DA

—— —— —— —— —— —— —— —— —— —— —— ——

DA

—— — —— — —— —— —— —— —— —— —— —— ——

D and A are both corners of the quadrilateral, but they are
not opposite corners. A diagonal connects opposite
corners. Reread and try again.

Figure 4.4. Interaction contained on a single frame (from Cook, 1984).

readily available. Paging back is often annoying, and there is always the possibility that while paging back, the student will forget
the question in the interaction. Third, memory demands may be
totally irrelevant to the instructional objective. For example, it is
imperative that a student be able to see a math problem while
working it; he or she does not need to memorize the problem, then
advance to the next screen and enter the answer.

Figure 4.4 illustrates the placement of text, response, and feedback on one frame.

If a frame contains text plus an interaction, a designer must
take care that the frame appears uncluttered. If the frame contains
interaction only, the designer must consider the influence of memory demands with respect to the instructional objective.

Displaying Text

Screen layout and composition are important in designing CBI.
The remainder of this section on student–frame interface is devoted
to guidelines for displaying text, tables, and figures.

Text refers to written words, phrases, and sentences. As mentioned earlier, special attention must be paid to the design of text
frames for computer screen display. The guidelines for display of
text are:

- Keep screen format consistent.
- Use uncluttered frames.
- Highlight important items.
- Write readable screens.

The Importance of Screen Consistency. Consistency refers to commonality in design, whether it be aspects such as functional area locations, type size, color, or codes used. If the format for each frame within each purpose is consistent, we predict quicker learning than if frames are not systematically designed. If the learner can easily recognize the purpose of each frame, he or she will not have to spend training time orienting to each frame. Thus consistency of design within any single purpose results in training-time economy. Consistency takes advantage of prior learning.

Examine the three frames in Figure 4.5. Notice that Figure 4.5B follows the same patterns established in Figure 4.5A. Notice also that the frame in Figure 4.5C does not follow the pattern, and your reading speed and comprehension probably decreased dramatically when you first examined Figure 4.5C.

Use of Uncluttered Frames. Another important principle in developing clear frames is to avoid cluttered, full-looking frames. A number of techniques can be used to avoid cluttered frames. These techniques include: liberal use of blank space; use of high-resolution

```
INTRODUCTION TO SCREEN DESIGN                    47/100

    Screens are divided into functional areas:
        *orientation
        *body
        *menu of options




    Where should the body of the frame begin?
    = =   Line 2

    INCORRECT. Line 2 is left blank.

HELP          MAIN MENU        BACK        NEXT
```

Figure 4.5A. Functional areas should remain consistent from frame to frame.

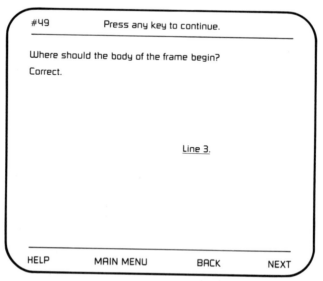

INTRODUCTION TO SCREEN DESIGN   48/100

Screens are divided into functional areas:

*orientation

*body

*menu of options

Where should the body of the frame begin?
□□◇ Line 3

CORRECT! The body begins on Line 3.

Figure 4.5B.   This frame's functional areas are consistent with Figure 4.5A.

#49   Press any key to continue.

Where should the body of the frame begin?
Correct.

Line 3.

HELP   MAIN MENU   BACK   NEXT

Figure 4.5C.   This frame's functional areas are not consistent with the two preceding frames.

graphics; breakup of cluttered frames into separate frames; use of windows; and use of upper- and lower case, without right justification.

Blank space may be used liberally. Much less information is presented on a computer frame than is presented on a page of printed text. In addition, the resolution is poorer on a computer screen than it is on a printed page. Blank space makes the screen cleaner looking. As Bork (1984) points out, blank space in a textbook costs money, but is nearly free on a computer screen. Blank space on text screens may be achieved with wide margins on all four sides of the screen, double spacing, and indents.

Another way to reduce clutter and increase screen clarity is to use a computer system with *high-resolution graphics*. Such a system creates sharp, clear print on the screen. This is achieved by purchasing special hardware and software for the computer. (Prices vary depending on the computer, but this equipment for a personal computer costs about $400.) Many educational computing centers have this equipment. Figure 4.6 shows how high-resolution graphics can be used to display complicated text and practice functional areas clearly.

Another technique is to divide a crowded frame into *multiple frames*. The frame in Figure 4.7 appears cluttered. The frame may be redesigned and made into two frames, as shown in Figure 4.8, to make it easier to read. The redesigned frames are not cluttered. They use blank space liberally. That there are more frames each with less information than the original frame is not a problem. In addition, the redesigned frames make use of consistencies in format across text presentation, text question, and answer frames that make reading these frames even easier.

Regarding multiple frames, however, as Heines (1984) notes, there are three drawbacks to converting single cluttered frames into multiple frames. First, some information fits together, and separating it arbitrarily for the sake of reducing clutter may be counterproductive. Second, short, choppy frames given an elementary, amateurish feel to the lesson. Finally, use of multiple frames encourages proliferation of frames without interaction. In summary, where multiple frames are used to break up a cluttered frame, care must be taken that the new frames are meaningful single frames.

Another technique useful in increasing the amount of information presented on one frame, and at the same time avoiding clutter, is *windowing*. A window is a screen area which is stored in memory and placed on an instructional frame to increase the amount of information presented on the frame. A window does not erase the information upon which it is overlaid.

Another window format, presented in Figure 4.9, involves six

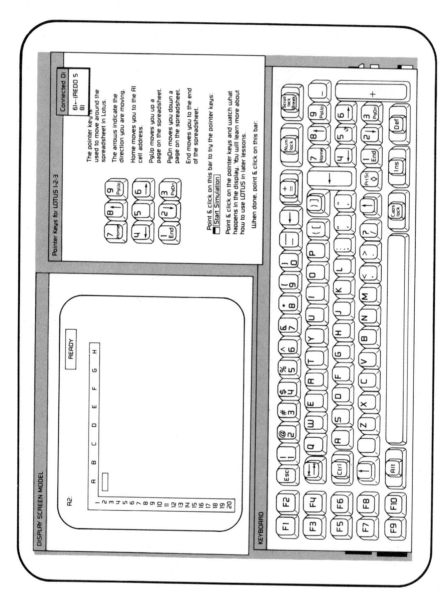

Figure 4.6. High-resolution graphics in CBI lesson on how to use LOTUS 1-2-3 (courtesy of Joseph Psotka, U.S. Army Research Institute).

92

```
  NUTRITION MODULE 2                    FRAME 18/35
  ─────────────────────────────────────────────────

  Carbohydrates supply the body with immediate calories.
  Carbohydrates provide the body with energy. Examples of
  carbohydrates include sugar, starchy vegetables, and fiber.
  Grain, nuts, potatoes, fruits, and legumes are high in
  carbohydrate.

  Which of the following is an example of carbohydrate? (Type
  in number of your answer). (1) Egg yolk, (2) Cashews,
  (3) Fish, (4) Liver ⌂    2         Correct. Cashews are
  high in carbohydrate.




  ─────────────────────────────────────────────────
  HELP        MAIN MENU        BACK        NEXT
```

Figure 4.7. A cluttered-looking frame.

windows, but they are not overlaid one on another. In this example, the student has been taught to attend to the windows in a certain order. The sequence requires the student to read the instructions, read the problem, determine from a list of information categories which one he or she needs to solve the problem, receive the information in the category, repeat the process if desired, ultimately solve the problem, and receive an evaluation of the solution. (Training in the sequence was done with four frames of instructions, all presented in the instructions window.) The interface in Figure 4.9 thus demonstrates a way to accomplish several different types of interactions, all on the same frame, in an uncluttered way.

Figure 4.10 shows a pull-down window that can be used to request a student status report. The report is displayed in the evaluation window, as shown.

One aspect of a window that is especially efficient is the fact that the window does not erase the screen underneath it. A window thus (1) avoids having to re-present any portion of the screen that would otherwise have been erased, (2) is programmed and stored without interfering with the lesson, and (3) does not interrupt the lesson visually (Heines, 1985). This is not the case with "viewports," which look like windows but erase the screen underneath (Heines, 1985).

Finally, *upper- and lowercase* and text without right justification increase clarity. It has been demonstrated that use of upper- and lowercase letters in computer frames makes for a more readable

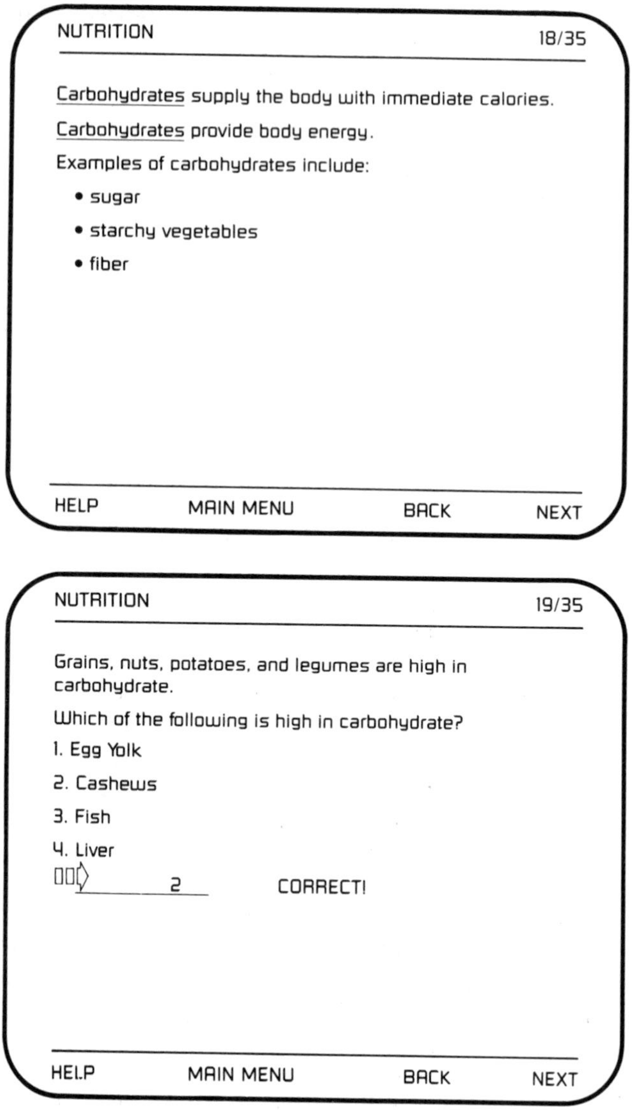

```
NUTRITION                                          18/35
─────────────────────────────────────────────────────

Carbohydrates supply the body with immediate calories.

Carbohydrates provide body energy.

Examples of carbohydrates include:

   • sugar

   • starchy vegetables

   • fiber




─────────────────────────────────────────────────────
HELP          MAIN MENU              BACK        NEXT
```

```
NUTRITION                                          19/35
─────────────────────────────────────────────────────

Grains, nuts, potatoes, and legumes are high in
carbohydrate.

Which of the following is high in carbohydrate?

1. Egg Yolk

2. Cashews

3. Fish

4. Liver
 □□◇        2            CORRECT!




─────────────────────────────────────────────────────
HELP          MAIN MENU              BACK        NEXT
```

Figure 4.8. Frame in Figure 4.7 redesigned.

frame than use of all uppercase (Reynolds, 1982). Captions and labels should be all uppercase (Galitz, 1981). The problem with using only uppercase letters is that readers are unaccustomed to that print style, and with all letters the same height, distinctions between letters are difficult. Reading speed is slowed as much as 13 percent when all uppercase is used (Galitz, 1981; Rehe, 1974). If you are constrained to use software that allows only uppercase

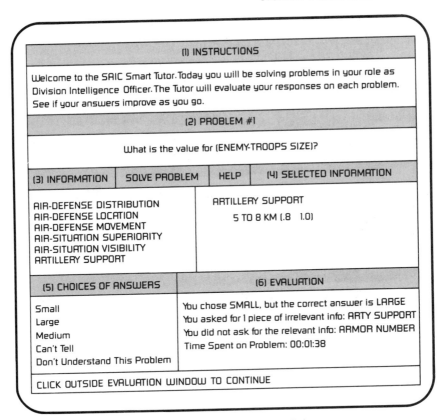

Figure 4.9. Windows used to accomplish complex dialogue.

printing, extra attention should be given to clearly indicating space between sentences and paragraphs.

Lines should be left- but *not right-justified*. Right justification is frequently accomplished by excessive word hyphenation at the end of lines and unusual spacing between letters and words. The impression of a right-justified computer frame is of an impenetrable, solid block (Reynolds, 1982). Word hyphenation at the end of lines should also be avoided. It is also important that every frame be self-contained. Sentences should end on the frame on which they begin.

Highlighting. In addition to using a consistent format that is free of clutter, a text frame should make clear those items that are important. (This principle of design is true for textbook material as well as computer frames.) Highlighting may be accomplished in a variety of ways. These ways include presenting important terms in uppercase letters, underlines, marginal notes, enclosing important material in a block, queries, and bulleted lists.

Pull Down Window

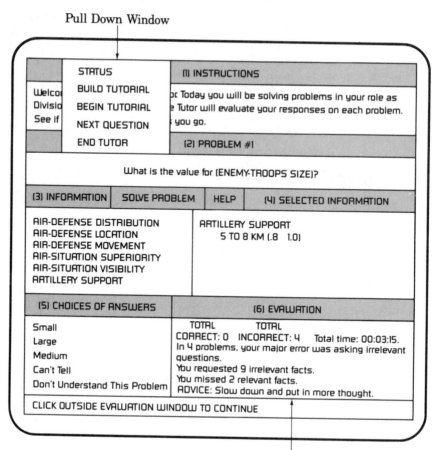

Student Status Report

Figure 4.10. Pull-down window can be used to request a summary student status report.

The sample in Figure 4.11 illustrates a highlighting technique where the important information is contained in a block. No doubt the query that might follow Figure 4.11 will ask about calcium, phosphorus, and abundancy in the body.

Some highlighting techniques should be used sparingly or not at all. Some computers have the capability to flash text on and off, but flashing text tends to interfere with concentration. Inverse video, where the letters are written in the same color as the background but blocked off in a contrasting color, can also be annoying.

Considerable care should be taken with use of multiple colors, each color coded to mean something different. Too many colors can break a student's concentration. Use of a few consistently used color codes, however, can be an effective display technique. Any design techniques that are used to emphasize important points should be understated. The emphasized point must remain distinguishable from the highlighting technique.

In summary, the principles of designing text frames presented above all relate to the overall ease with which a viewer interprets the frame. Consistent formats, uncluttered designs, and highlighting assist the viewer in making quick, correct interpretations.

Readability. A special concern related to the ease with which a frame is interpreted is the readability of the text. Several factors influence the student's reading comprehension of screen materials. These include: reading-grade level; wording, content, and context; sentence sequencing, and clear writing style.

The reading-grade level of a passage of text is calculated using any of a number of formulas (see Klare, 1974–1975, for a review). Many of these formulas are simple to use and calculate by hand. The basis of the formulas is the notion that reading-grade level is a direct function of average sentence length and word length in syllables. Use of readability formulas will indicate if the construction of a passage is suited to typical readers at a certain grade level. These simple formulas have been found to yield acceptable reading-grade-level estimates.

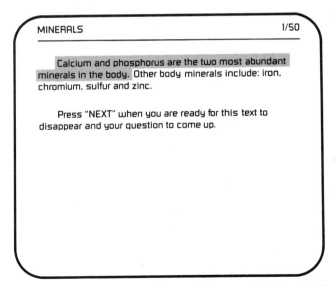

Figure 4.11. Illustration of a highlighting technique called "blocking."

One commonly used formula, the *Fog Index*, is calculated as follows:

1. Select a passage of about 100 words.
2. Calculate the average sentence length (i.e., the number of sentences in the passage divided by the number of words in the passage).
3. Count the words with three or more syllables.
4. Add the average sentence length to the number of three or more syllable words.
5. Multiply this sum by $4/10$. The product is the reading-grade level.

Some authors have written that in some cases simple reading-grade-level indexes are misleading. First, some difficult words (i.e., polysyllabic words), especially technical terms, may not be difficult for certain readers. In some cases, then, a simple readability index will yield an unfairly high estimate. For example, trainees in mechanics might not be expected to have difficulty reading and understanding such polysyllabic words as *carburetor, ignition, transmission,* or *combustion.* But other readers would have difficulty with those words.

Some computer programs for calculating readability consider baseline vocabulary of the reader. The Writer's Workbench is a comprehensive editing system which calculates readability relative to the readability of a standard passage (Macdonald, Frase, Gingrich, & Keenan, 1982).

A second influence on readability, in addition to reading-grade level, is the important interaction between wording and content. Even the simplest worded passage may be beyond comprehension if it presents content unclearly. Consider these sentences: "Subtract the left number. Put that number on the right. Put the first number on the left." No polysyllabic words, short sentences, no technical jargon, but beyond comprehension nevertheless.

A third factor in readability is context. Bransford and Johnson (1972) (also reported in Bransford, 1979) presented subjects with paragraphs of nine sentences of simple words, but the sentences made no sense taken together. Comprehension scores were low on the material. But when given the same paragraph plus an illustration that gave context to the paragraph, comprehension scores were high.

The final factor is clear writing style. Hallmarks of a clear style are use of brief simple sentences written in active voice. A topic sentence, containing a main idea, begins each paragraph. Explanatory sentences follow, then a conclusion.

Summary. In summary, four guidelines will help the courseware designer develop text frames that are easily interpreted by the student. First, functional areas of frames should remain consistent. Second, a frame should appear uncluttered. This is often accomplished by liberal use of blank space and use of windows. Third, highlighting important items assists the reader's interpretation of the material. Fourth, clearly worded, readable text should be displayed.

Text frame display and text frame content interact to produce high-quality, easily usable frames. In general, a high-quality series of text frames is a function of content properly sequenced for the instructional objectives, appropriate reading-grade level and clear wording, and frame layouts which are consistent, uncluttered, and highlighted.

Displaying Tables and Figures

A table is an information display arranged in columns. A figure is an information display which contains a picture, drawing, illustration, or graph.

Purposes of Tables and Figures. As described by Duchastel and Waller (1979), tables and figures in textbooks may serve any of three functions: attentional, explicative, or retentional. An *attentional* table or figure serves to hold the reader's attention and maintain interest. An *explicative* table or figure serves to present or explain what would be cumbersome in text. Any table or figure may also have *retentional* properties; often, visual images are more easily remembered than text passages. Certainly, tables and figures in courseware may assume any or all of these same three functions.

An example of an attentional figure in CBI might be a picture (if the capability is available) or other likeness of something related to the topic. Attentional figures not related to the topic might be used with young students, for example, a bumblebee or bear who is depicted as delivering instruction. When designing attentional figures, one should take care that the figure itself does not become more salient than the instruction. Overuse of attentional figures or exaggerated, brightly colored or flashing attentional figures may detract from the instructional sequence.

Designing explicative tables and figures for courseware requires some different techniques than those required for textbook tables and figures. Tables and figures appearing in textbooks often contain much information. Often, the information is abbreviated or is presented in symbols; thus the reader may dwell much longer on a table or figure than he or she would on a frame of text. In textbooks, information in tables and figures is not redundant with the text; text is used to explain or amplify information in tables and figures. Thus a reader may need to flip pages back and forth between table or figure and text. Since this procedure is awkward on a computer, special design and display techniques should be used.

CBI retentional figures and tables that aid memory of text material should relate to the text and emphasize it. Repeating figures from frame to frame increases emphasis.

Table and Figure Design in CBI. Tables and figures should be kept simple. Each table or figure should be clearly titled. Few, if any, codes should be used because legends might clutter the screen. Tables and figures should appear on screen before or simultaneous with text appearance. Presenting graphics while the student is reading is distracting (Galitz, 1981).

A table or figure might be self-explanatory and self-contained on one frame. If the table or figure is referred to in more than one frame, some means should be provided for repeating on subsequent screens all or portions of the table or figure.

The frames in Figure 4.12 show how to repeat a figure in a frame series instead of asking the student to page back to the original figure. The figure could also be repeated in a window. The figure is simple and uncluttered. The format of the figure is consistent across frames, and the topic of each frame is highlighted.

It is especially difficult to present figures such as complicated flowcharts on a computer screen. The figure may take up all the space on the screen and leave no room for instruction about the figure. Complex figures may be included in printed material that accompanies the courseware, and the student asked to look at the printed material while he or she completes the interactions at the computer. If it is critical to present a complex figure on a frame, the figure could be redesigned and presented on several frames. Presenting complex figures is less of a problem with high-resolution graphics.

The frames in Figure 4.13 provide an example of presenting text and tables in a CBI lesson for stockbroker trainees. The example also illustrates a good way in which the student can access needed information before an interaction. The student is allowed to choose what information he or she wants to see next. (If the student was only reviewing this problem, he or she might not want to look at everything again.)

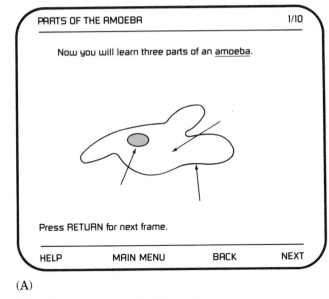

(A)

Figure 4.12A. Example of repeated figure in a frame sequence.

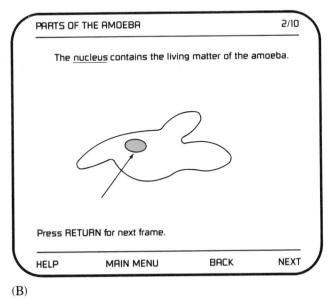

(B)

Figure 4.12B.

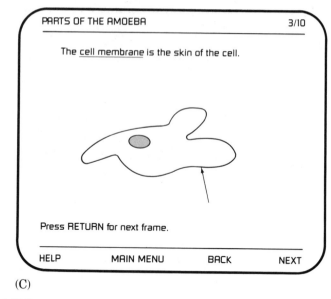

(C)

Figure 4.12C.

Student–Computer Dialogue

Dialogue Characteristics

Two student–computer dialogues are described in this section: menus and natural language. Most CBI systems interact with students through menus of options, student short answers to queries, and a student help-request feature. In a natural language system, the student and computer talk to each other in English sentences.

Interactive dialogues, including menus and natural language, may be described along several dimensions (Ramsey & Atwood, 1979). Of those dimensions described by Ramsey and Atwood, three dimensions are important for CBI dialogues. The dimensions are: initiative, flexibility, and power.

Dialogue initiative refers to the source of the conversation. In computer-initiated dialogue the student responds to computer prompts such as menus or test items. In mixed-initiated dialogue the computer can initiate dialogue but so can the student, who can ask a question even when no menu is present. The student can initiate dialogue through a request-help feature programmed on a special key of the keyboard or through a natural language query. Combinations of student- and computer-initiated dialogues are pos-

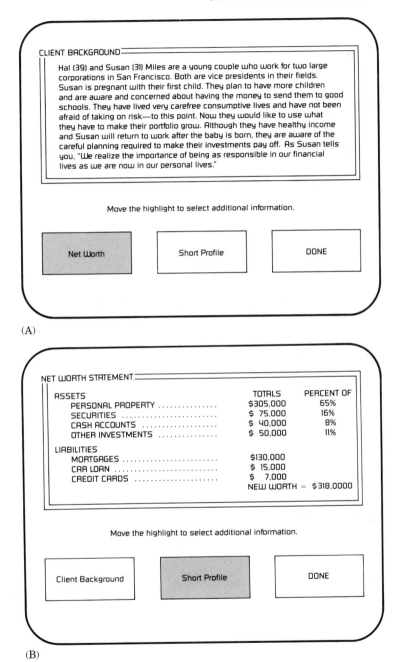

(A)

(B)

Figure 4.13 A,B,C. Frame sequence illustrating display of text, tables, and dialog. (Frames courtesy of Cathi D. Taggart, Merrill Lynch Training Division.)

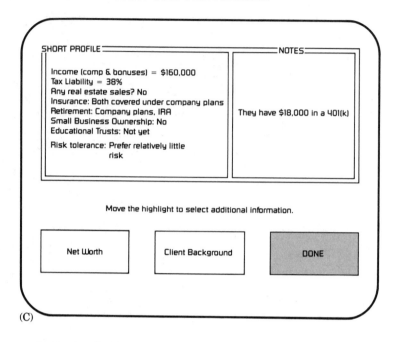

(C)

sible within a lesson, so a student could initiate dialogue only at certain points to make programming easier.

A *flexible dialogue* allows a student to query the computer in many ways. A menu-driven dialogue is inflexible if the appearance of the menu is out of the student's control or offers a limited number of options, or flexible if the menu may be produced easily or if the choices are extensive. A short-answer dialogue is flexible or inflexible depending on how well the computer responds to typographical errors. A natural language dialogue is flexible to the extent that it answers student questions in sentences or phrases and keeps the conversation going.

Dialogue power refers to the strength of a brief student entry. A powerful dialogue allows the student to request information with only a simple or brief entry. As Ramsey and Atwood (1979) note, too much power restricts the generality of the system. But at the same time, powerful student entries make easier an inexperienced student's encounter with the computer.

Menus

Certain characteristics of menus increase their initiative capability, flexibility, and power. The student should be given the capability to request help, exit the lesson, or return to the main menu, at any time during the lesson. Providing this capability allows for student initiative and is desirable in a CBI system.

Flexibility and power are discussed below in the context of menu design. Menu design involves five considerations: order of options, selection codes, menu layout, menu content, and control sequencing (Williges & Williges, 1984). The review by the Williges' covers human factors topics, not just menu design, for all computer systems, not explicitly instructional systems, and interested readers are encouraged to consult this excellent source. The information in this section has been taken from the Williges review and adapted to CBI.

Menu flexibility is increased by well-designed order of options, selection codes, and layout. As for order, menu options should be grouped or listed in a meaningful way. Groups of menu options should be clearly labeled with the group name. If options cannot be grouped, they should be listed in order of frequency of use.

The number of items a menu should contain depends on the size of the screen and the resolution of the type, but one column of menu items should have at most approximately five to nine items. Allowing a student to select an option by typing in the first letter or letters of the first word in the choice is preferable to having the student enter a, b, or c, and so on, which is arbitrary. For example, the student should be able to enter "y" for yes, not "a" for yes. If the items on the menu are numbered, the first item should be numbered 1, not 0. At least one space should be used between the item number and the item name.

As for menu layout, all menus should look alike in format. Figure 4.14 presents a menu format. The menu title and directions to the student should precede the list of options and should easily be distinguishable from the list. Menu choices should be listed in columns and left-justified. If two columns of items are used, the columns should be centered on the frame. If the number of options exceeds 10 to 15, the designer should construct a menu hierarchy, where selection of one item from the first menu list produces the set of items related to the selected item. This arrangement involves two screens. Any single menu should not exceed one frame.

Dialogue power refers to the effect created by selecting a useful option in as brief a manner as possible. Menu content and control sequencing are related to dialogue power. As for menu content, the options should provide useful choices to the student. The choices should be clearly worded. Choices in the form of a question should not be used.

Control sequencing refers to the system's ability to allow experienced students to skip over intermediate menus. For example, a

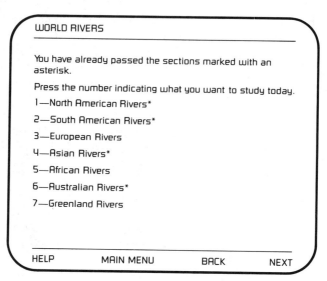

Figure 4.14. Menu format showing student instructions and list of options.

CBI system might use a three-level menu hierarchy. The first level might allow the student to select from four options: entering a lesson, review of lesson material, taking a test, or calling up the student performance record. These options might be numbered 1 through 4. If lesson entry is selected, the second level menu would allow the student to specify which lesson. These lesson options might be numbered 1 through 5. Then the third level menu would allow the student to specify the instructional objective desired, options numbered 1 through 5. A powerful system characteristic allows the experienced user to enter, for example, 1.3.4 at the first-level menu to indicate that entering lesson 3 at objective 4 is desired.

Natural Language Dialogue

A natural language dialogue has the ability to understand questions, commands, answers, metaphors, allegories, stories, and logical statements (Pask, 1984). The characteristics of a natural language CBI system include efficiency, habitability, tutorial capability, and handling of ambiguous responses from students (Burton & Brown, 1979). Efficiency refers to quick computer response time so that the student does not lose interest while awaiting further information. A habitable natural language system is one that understands a sufficient subset of the English language, including equivalent responses worded differently. The system should have a tutorial capability to teach a student why it cannot interpret a response. The system should answer student queries with unambiguous answers, even when asked an ambiguous question.

Natural language dialogues in CBI allow a student to converse with the computer concerning the topic under study. Natural language CBI systems are still in experimental stages.

Aronis and Katz (1984) developed a natural language instructional program called RICHARD which is based on discovery learning. The session begins with a computer-generated question, the system analyzes the student's answer, and eventually the system leads the conversation to touch on nine aspects which are considered important in teaching any topic. The nine aspects are formed by a 3×3 matrix: three perspectives by three types of information. The three perspectives are called particle or isolated, wave or included in a dynamic event, and field or abstract. Thus any topic may be considered in and of itself, related to other topics, or considered in the abstract. The three types of information concern contrasts or distinctive features, possible variations, and distribution of contexts applicable to the subject matter. Therefore, from any of the three perspectives, distinctive features, variations, and generality can be considered. Templates (specifications in the software) have been developed which extract keywords from the student's responses and determine which of the nine aspects is being studied. The system leads the student to master all nine aspects of the topic. The student is thus led to consider subject matter in depth.

Menu versus Natural Language

Experts differ concerning the desirability of natural language CBI, even though natural language CBI exists only in laboratories. Some believe that the flexibility of a natural language dialogue will benefit the learning process. Others believe that a natural language interface requires the student to do too much typing, whereas a menu dialogue requires little typing.

On the other hand, menu dialogues are often stilted, and when using the menu, the student may not be able to say what he or she wants to say. One recommendation for increasing flexibility of a menu dialogue is to make sure that a student can request help or exit the lesson at any point.

Intelligent Interfaces

A new concept, not yet implemented, in interface design is intelligent interfaces. An intelligent interface is one that adapts to the student. The intelligent interface selects what information to present and determines the best presentation format, based on unique characteristics of the student. Does this student prefer lists or narrative? Does this student like analogies? Does this student like to see several examples of a concept before going on to a generalization exercise? Does this student like "correct, good going," or "terrific?" Does this student do better with pie charts or bar charts? Does this student like menus with 5 or 15 items?

The intelligent interface will have three critical features (Halpin & Moses, 1987). One, it will know the student's goals and assess progress relative to those goals. Two, it will be able to predict correctly the behavior and preferences of any student based on past behavior and preferences. Three, the intelligent interface will be able to access other components of the computer system to help the student succeed.

Student–Performance Record Interface

Performance Record Purpose

The performance record should be designed based on its purpose. What is the performance record supposed to accomplish? How should this instructional stimulus be designed?

Student performance data reflect student mastery of the material. (This topic is discussed more in Chapter 8.) Student performance data help instructors (human or machine) determine when new material should be presented. Student performance data also help instructors assess the effectiveness of the courseware by pointing to sequences or lessons that might be too easy or too difficult, and thus in need of revision. Performance records allow students to keep track of their progress. Therefore, the purpose of student performance records is to help student and instructor make quick use of performance data, so that instructional decisions can be made. In addition, the performance record should be a clear archive of the instructional session.

Performance Record Design

Like displays described earlier in this chapter, displays of student performance data should be easily interpretable. Many student performance records violate most rules of clear presentation; implicit in their poor design is the notion that the information on the record is of little value. Words should be spelled out, not coded or abbreviated. Spacing and indentations help identify sections on the record. The student's name or identification should be included. Time and error scores for individual steps, clearly labeled, are helpful. Other performance measures and lesson totals are important. Graphs of student data clearly show progress and increase interest and motivation. Records of performance that are difficult to read will probably not be read; however, the motivational possibilities of well-designed records are important.

Some CBI systems include separate workstations (each with own display screen) for the student and instructor. These systems usually can display performance data at the instructor station on-line during the session. Thus the instructor can introduce the appropriate exercises into the student's lesson, as the instructor sees fit. (Having the computer make all the instructional decisions is simply too difficult to automate in many course content areas. In many complicated courses, instructors are just not able to state exactly how they know what to say and when to say it while teaching; too much judgment is involved, and the human teacher must therefore remain involved.)

Figure 4.15 presents an example of a clearly laid out on-line performance record, such as might be displayed at an instructor station during the session. The display presents student performance data and explicitly prompts the instructor to make instructional decisions.

When there is only one workstation, used by both student and instructor, student performance data are usually available only after the session. The sample in Figure 4.16 illustrates a readable performance record which provides helpful progress data after the session. The record provides information about the current session and allows one to track the student's history with the lesson.

The record in Figure 4.16 shows that on the date of the session, Sammy attempted the topic A test for the second time, and scored 90 percent correct. He also made two attempts at topic B, subtopic A. He did not do well, and ended the session. The record also shows that he attempted the lesson test during an earlier session, probably to see if he had already mastered the lesson. His score of 50 percent correct told him that he had better go through the

Student name: Sammy   Date of Session: 9-9-88

Student number: 1233

Lesson Name: Perceptual Thresholds

Topic A: Subtopic C

Frame	Instructional Objective	Start Time	Stop Time	Correct	Incorrect
10	Define term A	00:00	01:12	C	
20	Define term B	01:12	02:30	C	
30	Define term C	02:30	05:12		X
25	Remedial	05:12	06:37	C	
30	Define term C	06:37	07:06	C	

Can this student progress to a generalization exercise? Yes

Frame	Instructional Objective	Start Time	Stop Time	Correct	Incorrect
100	Generalization Subtopic C	07:06	10:12	C	

Figure 4.15. Sample student progress record displayed during CBI lesson, at instructor workstation.

lesson systematically. The record leaves blanks in the "percent correct" column for scores on the subtopics. This is because retries are allowed during the interactions. However, retries are not allowed during the tests, so the total number of tries is set. Thus a meaningful percentage can be calculated. This record does not calculate frequency correct and incorrect, but sufficient information is provided for the calculation.

Study Questions

Definition Questions

1. According to Galitz, what display characteristics do users appreciate?
2. What are some functions of computer frames?

Student name: Sammy	Date of Session: 9-9-88
Student number: 1233	Attempts this Session:
Lesson Name: Perceptual Thresholds	2nd Attempt—Topic A Test
	1st Attempt—Topic B, Subtopic A
	2nd Attempt—Topic B, Subtopic A

Topic/Subtopic	# Correct	# Incorrect	Time	% Correct	Attempts
Topic A	5	0	5 minutes	—	1st
Subtopic A	4	1	4 minutes	—	1st
Subtopic B	6	2	10 minutes	—	1st
Subtopic C	9	1	6 minutes	90	2nd
Test on Topic A					
Topic B	1	4	3 minutes	—	2nd
Subtopic A	Not	attempted			
Subtopic B	Not	attempted			
Test on Topic B	5	5	3 minutes	50	1st or earlier lesson
Lesson Test					

Figure 4.16. Sample student performance record for one session.

3. When designing multiple-function frames, how do you best divide the frame?
4. Describe Galitz's test for a good screen.
5. What are four guidelines for displaying text on a screen?
6. What are four factors that influence the readability of a text frame?
7. What are three important purposes of tables and figures?
8. What are the benefits of windows? Are there any drawbacks to using windows?
9. What are some guidelines for designing tables and figures on computer screens?

Discussion Questions

1. Why do you usually put less on a computer frame than you do on a book page?
2. Should a single frame serve single or multiple purposes? Explain.
3. When do you present complete interactions on a single frame? When do you present a single interaction on several consecutive frames?
4. What are some techniques for making important items readily distinguishable from less important items?

5. Design a menu allowing the student to answer the question "In what year did Columbus land in the New World?" Justify your menu and menu frame design.
6. What are the drawbacks and benefits of using menus and natural language dialogue?
7. How does one increase the initiative, ability, flexibility, and power of a menu interface?
8. Take an illustrated textbook. Turn to a short section, and design good computer frames for the section: five interactions and five frames with a table or figure. Be able to justify your frame design.
9. Design a student performance record (used after the session) to go along with your mini-lesson in Question 8.

CHAPTER 5

Sequencing Topics in CBI Lessons

The main topics in this chapter are:

- *Concept (topic) and task analysis*
- *Sequencing topics for concept lessons*
- *Sequencing procedural instruction*
- *Sequencing simulation exercises*
- *Learner versus program control of sequences*

Introduction

A CBI lesson is structured from the instructional objectives. First the designer determines the order in which topics and their instructional objectives are taught. Next the individual frames are written. Interaction frames are designed based on a determination of the specific antecedent and consequent events to be used in each interaction. The approach of constructing an overview sequence plan, then designing the individual frames is an example of a top-down approach to instructional design.

This chapter concerns determining the order in which topics are taught. Determining this sequence is a two-step process. First, the subject matter is analyzed to determine its components. This process is called topic or task analysis. A topic analysis is used for analyzing factual or conceptual information. A task analysis is used for analyzing step-by-step procedures. Second, the order in which the components will be introduced is determined. This process generates the overview sequence. Another concern during the design of the overview sequence is determining the parts of the sequence controlled by the student and the program. This concern is also covered in this chapter.

The process of overview sequencing described in this chapter is common to writing instruction for any medium. Sequencing simulation exercises and assessing learning versus program control are specific to CBI.

Procedures for Concept (Topic) and Task Analysis

A *concept* refers to a topic, information, knowledge, or idea, and a *task* or *procedure* refers to a step-by-step or chain activity. A *lesson of concepts* teaches facts and their applications, such as learning about geography, physics, or labels of component parts. A *procedure lesson* teaches a step-by-step activity such as typing, filling in a form (a common business training application), drawing a square, diagnosing a malfunctioning engine, or landing an airplane.

The distinction between concepts or knowledge and procedure is never clear-cut. Some CBI lessons may teach both concepts and tasks. Responding to topical or conceptual material includes a procedural component, such as typing in an answer or operating the computer. Procedural activity is obviously not accomplished without thought. However, the general distinction is helpful in sequencing a series of lessons as well as the main sections within a lesson.

Concept Defined

A concept may be defined simply as a unit of learning (Tiemann & Markle, 1983). A concept roughly equals an "idea," although many ideas contain several concepts. A concept is a group of stimuli that share a common property. Concepts have defining characteristics that include critical attributes and variable attributes (Tiemann & Markle, 1983). Each example of the concept possesses all the critical attributes of the concept; examples of the concept, however, may differ from each other along various dimensions or variable attributes. We can identify examples of a concept as well as nonexamples of a concept. This is done by comparing the characteristics of a potential example to the attributes of the concept of interest. A student has learned a concept when he or she can identify or discriminate examples from nonexamples. Proof of concept mastery can take many forms. (Recall the Chapter 3 discussion of the wide scope of possible instructional objectives for any one topic.)

On a very simple level, *flower* is a concept; all flowers possess a set of defining characteristics which distinguish them from other things. Flowers may differ from each other but still be classified as flowers. A toddler is said to know what a flower is when he or she picks a flower and not a leaf from a bush when asked to pick a flower, or answers "flower" when asked "What is this?" and the questioner points to a flower, and the child does not call a tree a flower.

On a more advanced level, *mitosis* is a concept that is defined by certain characteristics: a process of cell division; chromatin forms two sets of chromosomes; chromosomes split longitudinally; the single cell divides into two new daughter cells; each new cell has its own set of chromosomes. A student is said to know what mitosis is when he or she correctly selects or generates the set of defining characteristics of mitosis and is able to distinguish mitosis from other types of cell division.

Concept Analysis

Acquiring new knowledge is a cumulative activity. Thus topic analysis concerns listing the prerequisite knowledge that must be taught before the instructional objective can be met. Although there are some guidelines to follow, subjective judgment is required when determining exactly what knowledge is prerequisite. The judgment is based on an understanding of the student's history. Experience at topic analysis and teaching improves these judgments.

There are several ways of conducting a topic or concept analysis: identifying key terms, determining prerequisites, and listing defining characteristics of the topic. These approaches may generate similar topic analyses.

A concept analysis may be conducted by listing *key terms* in the content. For example, the key terms in the definition of mitosis include *cell division, chromatin, chromosomes, longitudinal, daughter cells.* Instruction in mitosis could systematically teach the definitions of each term by presenting defining characteristics, examples, nonexamples of each term, and requiring the student to interact with and learn the definitions of key terms. Figure 5.1 presents an example of a key terms concept analysis. Each term can become the topic of interactions. (For example, "Is this the definition of cell division?" "Fill in the blank in this definition of cell division." "Which of the following describes cell division?" "Which of the following is incorrect about cell division?" "Which graphic below illustrates cell division?")

A key terms topic analysis can be applied for an objective such as "Following the lesson about the Statue of Liberty, the student will answer correctly 19 of 20 questions concerning its size, location, costs, and history." The topic analysis for this lesson could consist

> *Mitosis* is a process of *cell division.*
> It results in the formation of two new cells,
>   each having the same number of *chromosomes*
>   as the *parent cell.*
> *Chromatin* forms two sets of chromosomes.
> *Chromosomes* split *longitudinally.*
> The single cell divides into two *daughter cells.*
> Each new cell has its own set of chromosomes.

Figure 5.1. Key terms that become interaction topics.

of a simple list of the facts (key terms) to be taught, grouped under the concepts that cover the lesson, such as *size, location, costs,* and *history.* Instruction about the size of the Statue of Liberty would present the dimensions of the statue, then require the student to interact with examples and nonexamples of its height, length, and so on. A sample interaction would be for the student to select which structure possesses the same height as the Statue of Liberty: the Eiffel Tower, World Trade Center, or a three-story apartment building.

Another method of concept analysis involves listing *skills and concepts prerequisite* to mastering the concept under study. This listing may be formatted as a concept hierarchy; an example is presented in Figure 5.2. The student should progress through interactions on each block in the figure. A concept hierarchy is based on the notion that learning is a sequential, cumulative, and hierarchical process. This method may be applied to lessons that teach sequential progressions of concepts.

A third method of concept analysis involves listing *critical and variable characteristics* of the concept. Figure 5.3 presents an example for a lesson on Gothic architecture. (The format of the figure is derived from Tiemann and Markle, 1985.) Each characteristic in Figure 5.3 is a topic for study. Thus the student goes through interactions on each characteristic listed in the figure.

How detailed should the topic or concept analysis be? Should you list key terms that define key terms and prerequisites of prerequisites? Judgment that develops from experience and knowledge of the learning histories of the students will help you determine how detailed a concept analysis is required. Generally, list all the new concepts and only those previously learned key terms, prerequisites, skills, or concepts that may need review.

CBI designers frequently take advantage of existing materials when conducting concept analysis. This can save time because it

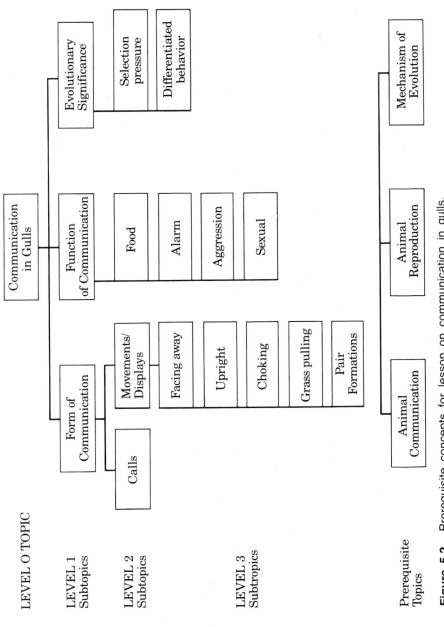

Figure 5.2. Prerequisite concepts for lesson on communication in gulls.

117

CONCEPT: GOTHIC STYLE

Critical Attributes:

1. Towers and spires for visibility
2. Continuation of vertical lines
3. Flying buttresses
4. Right angle, supporting piers

Variable Attributes:

1. Pointed arch
2. Ribbed groin vault
3. Lancet windows
4. Nave arcade

Teaching Examples:

1. Abbey Church of St. Denis, near Paris
2. Chartres Cathedral, Chartres
3. House of Jacques Coeur Bourges
4. Salisbury Cathedral, Salisbury

Teaching Nonexamples:

1. Imperial Palace at Goslac Lower Saxony (Romanesque Style)
2. St. Etienne Church, Caen (Norman Style)
3. Wartburg Castle, Eisenach (Romanesque Style)
4. White Tower London (Norman Style)

Figure 5.3. Critical and variable attributes of a concept.

gives the designer material to start with. In courses for new topics, the designer conducts the analysis using any written information available and interview time with an expert in the topic. When working with an expert, a designer might open with a question such as "What are the main ideas the CBI module should teach? What are the most important concepts that you apply in your work? What occupies most of your time? What topics should a student have mastered before attempting this topic?" (Sometimes, working with experts is challenging because they have little free time to spend with CBI designers. In addition, they may be great at doing their specialty, but not so great at talking about it. CBI designers have to respect both of those factors and develop ways to converse with experts that assist the experts to reveal important, pertinent information in as small an amount of time as possible.)

Task Analysis

Perhaps the easiest way to conduct a task analysis for a procedure is to perform the task yourself or watch someone perform the task and record everything you see. From your notes, you construct a task analysis. Tiemann and Markle (1983) propose listing an exact description of each step in the task, as well as exact descriptions of the environment involved in the task. This procedure will generate a task analysis such as shown in Figure 5.4 for a lesson in turning on the power to a volt-ohmmeter in a computerized training simulator. (Notice that this procedural lesson should be preceded by tutorial instruction in the terms used.)

Task analysis is an important part of government, business, and industrial training development. Those agencies and organizations develop instruction to teach hundreds of tasks and skills used by workers on the job. In addition to the simple task analysis procedure described above, numerous methods and systems which can become complicated (cf. McCormick, 1976) have been developed to

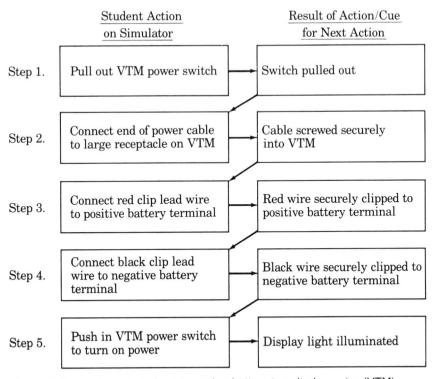

Figure 5.4. Task analysis for connecting battery to volt-ohmmeter (VTM) and turning on VTM power.

aid in the process of task analysis. Some of the other methods involve statistical analysis of the performance data of multiple individuals performing the same task, structured interviews of people who perform the task, as well as methods that seek to uncover the abilities required in each component task performance. The latter methods are based on the notion that teaching general skills is prerequisite to direct teaching of a specific task. Taxonomies of the skills and abilities underlying task performance are often used in business and industry (cf. Fleischman, 1984).

As was the case with concept analysis, the CBI designer does not necessarily start from scratch when conducting a task analysis for a CBI module. The economical designer will search for existing task analyses (e.g., a document that lists the steps in the activity) that might be used. For procedures that are common, this is often possible. If no information is available, the designer constructs the task analysis using available written material (may not be in step-by-step form) and expert consultation.

Sequencing Topics for Concept Lessons

Sequencing topics progresses from the concept analysis. The designer determines from the analysis if one sequence is strongly suggested or if any of a number of sequences might be used. The *key terms* concept analysis produces a list of terms. It may be the case that a single required sequence is not suggested. The subject matter might be presented in any number of ways, but some logical way is selected, usually based on the instructional designer's experience. Examples of sequences are chronological, smallest to largest, general to specific, and east to west. Another logical sequence might be gleaned from the reporter's maxim: who, what, when, where, how, and why. These topics follow a structure first, function second scheme. In the example in Figure 5.1, the broadest term, *cell division*, should be taught first, then the other terms in line with their order in the mitosis process.

How might you sequence the facts in the Statue of Liberty lesson mentioned earlier? A general guideline might be structure first, then function. First, describe the topic. Provide information about structure or physical appearance. If history is available, it might follow directly. Next, come the functions, first of the whole entity, then of each part. Finally, provide a summary.

Sequencing the lesson on communication in gulls (Figure 5.2) requires that the *prerequisite topics* have been mastered. This should be determined with a pretest. The first topic taught should be an introduction to communication in gulls (level 0), followed by a level 1 subtopic and its associated subtopics, then the next level 1 subtopic, and so on. The diagram in Figure 5.2 indicates that the level 1 subtopics can be taught in any order.

The *critical and variable attributes* concept analysis suggests that critical attributes be taught first, then variable attributes. The examples and nonexamples are used after the attributes concepts have been introduced.

For sequencing topics produced by any concept analysis, it is helpful to consider that knowledge is built on four hierarchical levels (Briggs & Wager, 1981; Gagne, 1977; Becker, Englemann, & Thomas, 1975). The levels in order are: discrimination, concepts, rules, and problem solving. If you can match topics in the topic analysis to those levels, you should teach in order from discriminations to problem solving.

A student who makes a discrimination can tell if two stimuli are the same or different. Discriminations are taught first. Next examples and nonexamples of concepts are taught. Using concepts already learned, rules can be taught. When a student uses a rule, he or she takes a set of concepts and generates examples and nonexamples of the set of concepts. In later lessons on problem solving, a student takes two or more rules and generates a solution, or a stimulus in the set of stimuli formed by the intersection of the rules. Becker, Englemann, and Thomas (1975) suggest that instruction for the very young students usually teaches discriminations and concepts, and instruction for older students usually emphasizes multiple concept use and problem solving.

Sequencing Topics in Procedural Lessons

Two factors should be considered in sequencing steps in a procedural CBI lesson. One concerns how much of the sequence should be presented in one lesson; a designer should select between whole- and part-task sequence plans. A second consideration is whether the steps should be presented in forward or backward sequence. A forward sequence, from first to last step, is usually used. However, there are some instances where it may be useful to present steps in a procedure in a backward manner, last step first, then second to last step, and so on. These considerations are described below.

Whole- and Part-Task Training

Using a *whole-task* plan, individual parts of a skill are practiced in sequence, and the entire sequence may be practiced before any component is mastered. For whole-task CBI lessons, it is usually desirable to select a task that can be performed completely during each instructional session. The procedure should have few enough steps that going through the procedure will not exceed the expected length of the instruction session.

A whole-task plan might be used in a lesson to teach a job procedure such as filling in an order form that contains only 15 blanks. The student could practice filling in the form completely in one session. The student would continue through the form even if errors were made on certain blanks. Mastery in completing blank 1 is not prerequisite to attempting to fill in blank 2, and so on. A whole-task plan increases the student's sense of context and provides reinforcement for completion even at the first lesson.

Using a *part-task* plan, individual parts of the task are mastered before the total task is attempted. This method is appropriate where the task is complex, easily broken down into discrete components, with each component containing few enough steps that the component may be completely performed in one session. Use of a part-task plan prevents the student from quickly performing the entire task, but probably reduces errors that would be made in performing a complicated task all at once from the beginning.

Forward Chaining

Most CBI lessons that teach tasks or procedures are conducted using a forward-chaining procedure. Forward-chaining procedures should be used (1) when the steps must be performed in a forward fashion because later stages depend on the completion of earlier steps, and (2) for certain sequences which are arbitrary but accepted by convention.

Teaching an employee to fill in an order blank that leads to the calculation of a grand total for amount due illustrates the first case in which forward sequencing should be used. Customer identification and shipping information usually goes at the top of the form, then the items ordered, unit cost per item, quantity per item ordered, subtotal price, tax, shipping, and grand total are calculated. Each step in the calculation must be completed before the grand total is calculated. The sequence of steps is not arbitary in this case; the grand total must be calculated in a specific way.

Backward chaining could not be used because the blank for the grand total cannot be filled in first.

An example of the second case is the way we learn the alphabet. We learn *a*, then *a-b*, then *a-b-c*, not *z*, *y-z*, then *x-y-z*. The sequence of letters in the alphabet is arbitrary, although accepted by convention. This type of sequence is taught in a forward manner.

One laboratory study (K. M. Weiss, 1978) compared a forward (part-task)-chaining procedure to a backward (part-task)-chaining procedure on a task with arbitrary sequencing. Ten subjects learned four six-link response chains, two chains in a forward manner and two chains in a backward manner. The chain was an arbitrary series of six button presses on a display panel. In the backward procedure, the last button press, number 6, was reinforced with points that could be traded for money. After press 6 was mastered, the next-to-the-last press was added so that the subject now had to make two correct presses, 5 and 6, to get points, and so on. In the forward procedure, the first press taught was the first in the chain, number 1. Once mastery was attained, the subject had to make two correct presses, 1 and 2, to earn points. The study found that the forward procedure produced many fewer errors than the backward procedure.

In this study, the forward procedure produced the terminal reinforcer (points) before the entire chain was learned. Because of this, the procedure may be called part task. Usually we think of only the last link in the chain as producing the terminal reinforcer, with intermediate steps cueing other steps. Thus the forward and backward procedures were equal with respect to number of reinforcers used. The key press sequence was not a true chain, but was a series of independent steps abritrarily linked by the experimenter. A forward whole-task procedure where press 1 produced only the cue for press 2, but not points, might have yielded different results. Nevertheless, this study suggests that for independent steps arbitrarily linked, a forward sequence may be valuable.

Backward Chaining

In backward chaining, the last link or component skill in the chain is taught first because the last step produces the terminal reinforcement. That reinforcement is task completion. Once that step is mastered, the next-to-the-last step is added so that now two steps must be performed before the task is completed. Those two steps are practiced in sequence until mastery is reached, then the next step back is added, and so on, until the entire chain is mastered.

A common example of a backward chaining procedure is the way many of us were taught to tie our shoes. Our early attempts to complete the entire sequence in a forward manner produced groans and frustration. So our parent or sibling would complete most of the tie; then all we had to do was pull through the final loop. As we mastered each step, more and more steps were added backward until we mastered it all.

One controlled study in this area compared forward (whole task) and backward (part task) procedures in an aircraft training simulator used to teach dive bombing (Bailey, Hughes, & Jones, 1980). All 20 subjects saw a videotape of the complete task from start to finish. The steps in the task were: fly downwind, fly the base leg, roll-in, and final leg. Subjects in the backward procedure group practiced the task in a standard backward-chaining manner. Subjects in the forward group practiced the entire chain to completion. Subjects in the backward chaining group met training criteria significantly faster and showed greater accuracy on test trials than subjects in the whole-task group. The chaining procedure worked well with a task whose components are necessarily sequential, not arbitrarily linked. [An interesting comparison would have been a forward (part-task)-chaining group which obtained the same number of completions or reinforcers as the backward-chaining group.]

A more recent study found that backward chaining (part-task) produced better performance on a test task of simulated carrier landing than did forward-chaining (whole-task) procedures (Wightman & Sistrunk, 1987). Training that simplified the task, by means of decreasing simulated aircraft weight to increase aircraft responsiveness to throttle adjustments, did not have a beneficial effect.

Sequencing Simulation Exercises

Difference Between Simulations and Tutorials

CBI tutorials for teaching concepts and procedures introduce new material and provide practice. Tutorials advance students through acquisition and fluency building to mastery. Some tutorials also provide generalization practice, and some may be used for mastery maintenance.

Simulations provide for trial-and-error learning and generalization practice. They permit students to apply concepts already acquired in tutorials or through other media. Simulations foster new learning, not in a step-by-step fashion as is the case with a tutorial, but through student discovery. Students practice what they have learned in a variety of applications.

Because even simple tutorials can and should provide generalization practice (discussed more in Chapter 7), costly simulations are usually developed for adult students to practice complex skills. Simulations often involve use of color and computer graphics. Some employ computer or videodisk technology which allows students to take action on filmed still and moving sequences. Simulation development is expensive and is therefore undertaken when poor human performance in "real life" would lead to major problems.

Sequencing in Simulations

Determining the order in which to present practice exercises within a simulation is based on difficulty. Most simulations present practice exercises of equal difficulty, one by one. Others present exercises of increasing difficulty, from easy to more difficult. Sequencing in tutorials is more complex than sequencing in simulations, because any of a number of sequencing plans can be selected for tutorial sequencing.

Sequencing in Single-Skill-Level Simulations

Simulations are difficult to design and program. Most simulations provide practice for one skill level. Situations or exercises of similar difficulty are presented, one at a time, and the student responds to each situation. Each new situation requires the student to use skills previously learned, but the student gains experience by solving each situation.

An example of a single skill simulation would be a simulation that provides practice in calculating the location of a moving target, given the target's continuously changing location. To keep the difficulty level constant, the number and timing of location changes would have to be kept constant. The student would compute expected path based on course changes. The student would enter an expected location and be told if that location could be correct. The student would practice over and over until criteria for speed and accuracy are met.

In single skill-level simulations, then, the CBI designer constructs multiple practice exercises of equal difficulty, and the simulation presents them one at a time. The student controls the pace of the exercise because the next exercise is available as soon as the previous one is completed.

Better simulations keep track of a student's performance over time. Performance should become quicker and more correct with practice. Better simulations are able to diagnose performance problems and report these to the student.

Sequencing in Multiple-Skill-Level Simulations

In a multiple-skill-level simulation, the student encounters practice exercises that increase in difficulty. These exercises allow the student to practice multiple skills, from simple to complex skills. Factors that increase the difficulty of simulation exercises include the number of unknown bits of information that the student requires in order to solve the problem, multiple factors for the student to consider in solving the problem, and time constraints. The CBI designer sequences practice exercises in order of increasing difficulty in a multiple-skill-level simulation. In this way, a student's generalization responses can be systematically shaped by the CBI.

An example of a simulation with exercises that increase in difficulty is the one presented earlier, in Figure 1.3. The student is required to make predictions, based on an increasing number of pieces of information. The easy exercises come first, those that the student can solve using one bit of information. The more difficult exercises require that the student base the solution on as many as 17 pieces of information.

Learner- versus Program-Controlled Sequences

Whether conceptual, procedural, or simulation activities are designed, the CBI designer plans a sequence of instruction as described earlier in this chapter. However, a second sequencing issue arises in CBI. Should the learner be forced to study in the designed sequence (program controlled sequence), or should the student be allowed to determine what topic to study next? In addition, should the CBI allow the student to select other options, such as number of practice interactions attempted, number of examples or nonexamples presented per concept or rule, and length of session?

Many designers have computer systems which enable them to present both program- and learner-controlled sequences. A list of pertinent questions that the CBI designer answers when determining sequences includes:

- Should the courseware present the same linear sequence of instruction to each student?
- Should the learner be allowed to select the topic sequence, pace, amount of instruction, amount of practice, and length of session?
- Should the sequence be responsive or adaptive to learner aptitudes, past achievement, pretest scores, or on-line performance?
- Should a combination strategy be used in which the program advises the learner of an optimal sequence based on previous progress and on-line needs, and then lets the learner decide whether to follow that prescribed course?

Topic Sequencing

Research findings provide guidance in deciding if the learner or program is better for determining instructional sequences. Steinberg (1984) writes that both learner and program control may be effective, depending on the maturity of the learner and the difficulty of the content. She suggests that learner control is acceptable for mature students if (1) the instructional program is supplementary, (2) its completion is voluntary, or (3) if the content is easy, even if mastery is mandatory. On the other hand, she suggests program control for less mature students where completion is mandatory or for any student if the content is difficult.

Number of Examples per Rules

Ross and Rakow (1981) compared linear (nonadaptive) program control, adaptive (tailored to the student) program control, and learner control methods in a computer-managed course. Five introductory mathematical rules were taught. The number of examples given per rule was varied depending on the teaching method used. In the nonadaptive course, five examples per rule were given. This number had previously been found to be an optimal number of examples per rule. In the adaptive program control course, the number of examples was adapted to the student's pretest score. Students with higher pretest scores received fewer examples per rule than students with lower pretest scores. In the learner control course, a minimum of two examples per rule was given. However, students were told that they could request up to six more examples per rule, depending on how well they felt they knew the rule.

Results indicated that adaptive program control produced better performance than did the other procedures. Noteworthy was the fact that adaptive control was more effective with low pretest scorers. High pretest scorers were less affected by the different procedures. The data also showed that students in the learner control group requested fewer examples and spent less time in training than in other groups, but with resultant decrement in scores.

In a related study, Ross (1984) adapted the number of examples given per rule based on the student's ability rather than past achievement in the topic. Ability measures were taken from short ability tests. This method of adapting instruction compared favorably to several nonadaptive methods also used in the study. It is interesting that one nonadaptive program control method, where 10 examples (a high number) per rule were presented, produced poor performance. The author speculates that such a high degree of instructional support, unwarranted for many learners, resulted in an inefficient use of training time and boredom.

Tennyson and Buttrey (1980) studied a method of adaptation called program advisement. In this method, the student is given advice about an optimal sequence; the student may choose to use or ignore the advice. According to Tennyson and Buttrey, program advisement includes any of four types of advice: (1) how the student initial performance level compares to the desired performance level; (2) the optimal amount and sequence of instruction; (3) based on the initial performance level, an on-line progress record, updating the student's distance from the goal; and (4) on-line updated instructional sequence advice.

Learner and program control methods were compared, with and without program advisement. The learners were high school students who were taught eight concepts in psychology. The computer-management system determined the number of examples given per concept to each student. This number was based on the individual's pretest achievement level and was revised on-line to reflect student progress. In the learner control conditions, students selected the number of examples they wished to study. Advisement consisted of suggesting the number of examples needed to reach mastery. This number was derived individually based on performance.

Results indicated that computer adaptive control procedures were superior to learner control procedures for teaching these concepts. Advisement improved both learner and program control procedures. Learner control without advisement produced the poorest results. As found in other studies, students in the learner control group spent less time in instruction and requested fewer examples, to the detriment of their scores.

Program Adaptations

If the program adapts to learner performance, should it adapt to preselected measures of ability (e.g., aptitude) or to measures of performance (e.g., achievement) for the topic under study? Ross (1984) has studied the differences between aptitude and achievement adaptations. Ability was measured in standardized tests administered before instruction, and achievement in the topic of study measured during a pretest in which the information of interest was tested directly. Ross (1984) states that adaptations based on achievement produce more favorable results.

Other studies have found other ways to provide adaptations in the delivery of CBI. One is adaptation of the context of the material to the background of the student (Ross, 1983). For example, nursing students performed better following instruction in nursing concepts presented in a nursing context. The students did poorer when the same concepts were presented abstractly.

Self-Pacing

Self-pacing has two meanings in CBI. First, any CBI session is self-paced in the sense that the speed and accuracy of a student's interactions with the computer determine how long it takes the student to complete the lesson. This self-pacing is inherent in the nature of the interaction. Total program control of within-session pace would prevent learning because the program would not wait for the student response, the lesson would not progress based on response accuracy, and it would not allow the student to select the next topic for study.

The second meaning of self-paced is much broader and refers to the freedom given to the student to schedule CBI sessions, report for sessions, and complete the lesson. The student is usually given a deadline for completion, but the deadline is often weeks away. Self-pacing, a method of learner control, could be a desirable way to teach independent learning for students of all ages. For older students, self-pacing allows students to balance their own schedules. However, students with control over instructional pacing often perform poorly. Courses that allow self-pacing often result in procrastination and high withdrawal rates. Johnson and Ruskin (1977), in a text based on reviews of instructional design literature, report that procrastination in self-paced courses has detrimental effects, which include:

• Decrease in probability of course completion

- Decrease in probabillity of obtaining high grade
- Increase in probabillity of withdrawal
- Increase in probability of fear, frustration, and anxiety

Johnson and Ruskin explain that students who procrastinate or withdraw are not necessarily poor students. They cite a Born and Whelan (1973) study which found that 80 percent of withdrawing students had passed their last quiz, and 76 percent had satisfactory scores before withdrawing. Johnson and Ruskin find that students who withdraw have simply not taken enough unit tests; they fall further behind as time passes. Effective self-pacing may be difficult for the many students who do not have much experience with it.

Johnson and Ruskin suggest some positive consequences that might be used in self-paced courses to reinforce unsteady progress. These include opportunity to take an early final exam, or even exempt the final exam if progress is steady, public or private posting of individual progress charts, and extra points for maintaining steady or ahead of schedule progress. Negative consequences for unsteady progress, such as an F grade for a poor schedule, produce high withdrawals and low enrollments.

Summary of Learner Control of Sequence versus Program Control

Studies indicate that program control of sequence, which adapts to student performance, is associated with better student performance than is nonadaptive program control or learner control. Students who make their own decisions about what and how much to study in a CBI course often do not study enough.

In courses where topics need not be studied in a particular order, or for easy courses, students may be given the choice about what topic to study next. (For example, from Figure 5.2, the student could select topic order for the three level 1 subtopics.) But the program should control topic sequencing for difficult courses. In addition, the program should control the number of interactions attempted by the student, adapting the number to student performance. If the course permits the student to control the number of interactions attempted (perhaps to give older students a sense of freedom), the program should at least advise the student about an optimal number and display an on-line progress record for the student.

The length of a single CBI session is controlled by the speed and accuracy of a student's responses, not by the program. A single session moves as quickly as the student does. Pacing over multiple sessions, however, should not be left up to the student. The program or teacher should schedule intermediate deadlines for completion of a long course to prevent students from falling behind.

Study Questions

Definition Questions

1. What are three general techniques used to conduct a concept analysis?
2. What is a general technique used to conduct a task analysis?
3. What is the difference between whole- and part-task lesson planning? When should each be used?
4. What is the difference between backward and forward chaining? When should each be used?

Discussion Questions

1. Define *concept analysis* and *task analysis*. Why is it important to conduct a concept or task analysis when designing instruction?
2. How does a CBI designer determine the sequence of topics in a lesson? subtasks in a task lesson? exercises in a simulation?
3. How are tutorials and simulations alike, and how are they different?
4. Who should control the sequence of instruction, the student or the program? Explain.
5. What are examples of adaptations that can be made to the instructional sequence that tailor the sequence more toward the student?
6. Who should control the pace of instruction within a session, the student or the program? Explain.
7. Who should control the pace of scheduling instructional sessions, the student or the system? Explain.

CHAPTER 6

Writing Introductions, Interactions, Remedial Branches, Reviews, and Tests

The main topics of this chapter are:

* *Writing introductions*
* *Design of interactions*
* *Design of remedial sequences*
* *The importance of review*
* *Reliability and validity in CBI tests*

Introduction

After the topic/task sequence is constructed (as described in Chapter 5), the individual frames for each topic/subtopic and task/subtask are designed. The types of frame content needed are introductions, interactions, remedial sequences, reviews, and tests. Designing these frames is the focus of this chapter. The design of interaction frames is based on learning principles, and these are discussed in the section on interactions. Table 6.1 presents the outline for a detailed sequence. (This outline was presented originally in Chapter 3.)

Introduction Frames

The lesson introduction sets the stage by briefly presenting the topics to be covered. The instructional objectives are presented. The introduction often recalls previously learned material (as an "ad-

132

TABLE 6.1 Detailed Courseware Plan

Topic X
  Introduction to Topic X
  Subtopic 1
    Introduction to subtopic 1
    Interaction: Identify A   Remedial frames
    Interaction: Identify A   Remedial frames
    Interaction: Define A   Remedial frames
    Review of subtopic 1
    Test of subtopic 1   Contingent branch
  Subtopic 2
    Introduction to subtopic 2
    Interaction: Define A   Remedial frames
    Interaction: Identify B   Remedial frames
    Interaction: Define B   Remedial frames
    Review of subtopic 2
    Test of subtopic 2   Contingent branch
  Subtopic 3
    Introduction to subtopic 3
    Interaction: Apply A   Remedial frames
    Interaction: Apply B   Remedial frames
    Review of subtopic 3
    Test of subtopic 3   Contingent branch
  Topic X Test
    Review of subtopics 1, 2, and 3
    Test of subtopics 1, 2, and 3
    Present total score and prescription
  Repeat for each topic in the lesson

vance organizer") to create a context for the new material. The introduction also gains the student's attention and creates interest. Introductions are important antecedent stimuli.

The frames in Figure 6.1 illustrate a lesson introduction. These frames present objectives, recall related material, and create interest. Introductions need not be confined to a single frame. Placing new material in context is an aid to learning.

Interaction Frames

Interaction is the critical component of CBI. Interaction provides the opportunities for the student to respond to new instructional challenges. Reinforced interaction is a teaching component, used as an exercise preliminary to testing, which may or may not provide

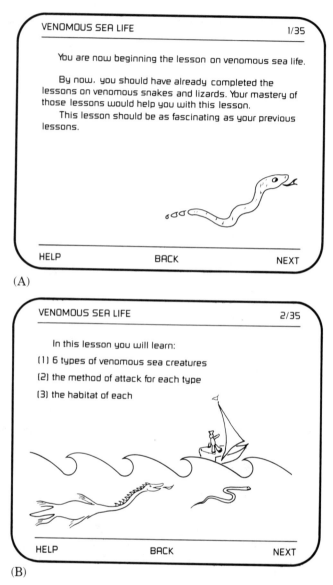

Figure 6-1. Introduction frames for a lesson.

immediate feedback for each response. Interaction is the time for students to practice the material.

Often a student's scores in interaction are of less interest than scores in tests, but interaction is the time the student learns the material. Interaction practice precedes testing. Amount or quality of performance in interaction or practice is sometimes not recorded, but interaction scores are helpful in CBI evaluation. Troublesome or very easy interactions need to be reworked.

Learning Principles for Interactions

An overview of learning theory was presented in Chapter 2. To design interactions, more detailed information is needed. Behavior shaping and generalization are the learning processes involved in interactions. Behavior shaping concerns the establishment of new learning, and generalization concerns the application of that learning to new situations. Knowledge of these processes underlies the CBI designer's selection of which antecedent events (e.g., lengthy or brief instructions, large or small units, stories or lists) to present. An introduction to behavior shaping is presented in this chapter, as well as a discussion of antecedent and consequent events which are critical to shaping. Details about tailoring antecedent and consequent events for student performance levels, including generalization, are presented in Chapter 7.

Behavior shaping is the process of teaching a student something new. The shaping process molds and encourages new responses by working on responses which are not yet correct. Shaping is accomplished by gradually changing antecedent and consequent events. A knowledge of how to shape is critical in developing effective CBI. The sequence of frames and activities in CBI shape or teach new information if the sequence is well designed.

Shaping occurs in three steps. First, a response is obtained from the student. Second, the student perfects the response. Third, fewer or less explicit antecedent and consequent events are presented so that the sequence of antecedent stimulus–response becomes more fluid.

As for *antecedent events in CBI,* the way to get the student first to try a new skill or give the first answer to questions about new information is to ask for it directly. The request is simple, such as "Please enter your answer." If the response still does not occur, the direction may be made more elaborate, such as "Remember the three rules. Now, please enter your answer." This elaboration, called a *prompt,* functions as a new antecedent event. Then, as soon as the student responds, a reinforcer is presented. Even if the response is incorrect, a reinforcer may be presented just for the attempt, such as "Incorrect, but nice try," especially if the student hesitated before answering.

Next, more accurate responses are encouraged. The antecedent events, prompts, and directions are changed; for example, "That was close. This time, try to get both the hundreds and tens."

Prompts are dropped out or *faded* until the correct response is obtained without extra help.

It is important in CBI to provide the student an initial chance to respond correctly with minimal assistance from the antecedent event. If the student responds correctly, prompts do not have to be given and then faded, thus saving training time.

Once a response is entered into the computer, the computer judges the response against some criterion. The acceptable parameters of the response (e.g., how close to perfect the response has to be; the time limit, if any, on the response) are determined by the CBI writer and incorporated by the computer programmer into the courseware.

Based on the assessment of the response, a *consequent event* occurs. If the response is correct, or correct enough, the consequence (or *reinforcer*) should increase the likelihood that in similar circumstances the student will give the same correct answer again. If the student's response is not correct, the consequence (*punisher*) should decrease the likelihood that the student will err again. Learning theory is more developed for consequent events in CBI than for antecedent events. There are several types of consequent events; these are described below.

A *reinforcer* is a consequent event that encourages a response to occur again. Two types of reinforcers are described below: positive and negative. Natural positive reinforcers are also described.

Positive reinforcers (also called reinforcing consequences or reinforcing stimuli) in instructional material are given after the student's response and tell the student that his or her answer was correct. Examples of commonly used positive reinforcers in CBI are word messages such as "correct," "fantastic," or "Yes" with the correct answer restated.

Reinforcers do not have to be word messages. Pleasing graphics or musical tones may be used as reinforcers in CBI. Another type of potential reinforcer is pleasurable activity. In CBI, activities such as games or rest after some amount of work might be used as reinforcers. The range of reinforcers possible appears to be larger and easier to implement in CBI than in other instructional media.

Reinforcers vary from student to student. One student's answers may be reinforced by word messages such as "Good job," but for the same student, pleasant tones may have no reinforcing effect at all. The exact opposite might be true for another student. It may also be the case that for a certain student, "Good" has a reinforcing effect, but "Wow, you're the greatest" has no effect, or worse yet, may have a detrimental effect. Five minutes of a video game may reinforce some students' responses, but other students may have no interest in video games. An adult might become angry at a lesson that continually said "Wow, you're the greatest," but the same message might be motivating to a child.

For many students, word messages are suitable CBI reinforcers. Many of us are used to receiving verbal praise for good work, and verbal praise has long been an effective reinforcer. Graphics, music, and games, all possible in CBI, have been less commonly used as reinforcers in the pasts of many students. It is possible to turn things that are not reinforcers into reinforcers, but doing so is often complicated. Perhaps the best rule of thumb is to consider your audience. Ask questions such as:

* How old are the students?
* How have the students performed in training when the "usual" reinforcers have been used?
* What do they like to do? to hear? to see? to cause?

Knowing your audience will help you select CBI that uses reinforcers appropriate to the students, and will help you select reinforcers to use in CBI that you might write.

Other commonly used terms for positive reinforcement are feedback, positive feedback, or knowledge of results. However, using strict definitions, positive feedback and reinforcers are not the same things. Positive feedback may not always be reinforcing. If positive feedback is reinforcing (i.e., causes the correct response to occur again), it becomes a type of reinforcer. Reinforcers are the larger category; positive feedback (which is truly reinforcing) is a subset of reinforcers.

Natural reinforcers occur simply as the result of completing a task. Learning is said to occur "naturally" if reinforcers are derived from performing the behavior. For many people, simply operating a computer provides natural reinforcement because the person's computer operating is reinforced by its effects on the computer—it quickly becomes unnecessary for another person to congratulate the computer user, to assure that the person will continue using the computer.

The following is an example of natural reinforcement in CBI. The student is learning to repair an engine. The engine is connected to the computer, and if the student replaces the correct valve, the engine roars. The roaring engine is a sign of a correctly completed task, a natural reinforcer.

Natural reinforcement, in the form of satisfaction, can occur frequently in CBI. Occasionally, students can be asked to check their own answers. For example, the question "Does your answer match the correct one?" can be answered by the student with an enthusiastic "yes." Such a technique fosters the development of natural reinforcement.

Negative reinforcers, like positive and natural reinforcers, increase the likelihood that a certain response will occur again, but they accomplish this differently. A negative reinforcer is an unpleasant stimulus that is removed if the student gives the correct answer. Thus negative reinforcers work because of threat. A student works to get the right answer so that he or she can escape or avoid something unpleasant.

The following is an example of negative reinforcement in CBI. An obnoxious tone is presented and the student told that correct answers will turn off the tone. Obviously, this would create a stressful learning environment. Negative reinforcers often lead to negative emotional responses by students. It is best not to buy or write courseware based on negative reinforcement.

The *timing of reinforcers* is important in CBI. Must a reinforcer be presented after every correct response? How soon after the response should the reinforcer be delivered? Scientific studies have shown that learning progresses differently depending on how many or what percentage of responses are reinforced. For example, the effects may be different if you reinforce every response than if you reinforce every tenth response. A rule of thumb is that you should reinforce every correct answer when the student is first learning something new. This is called *continuous reinforcement.* As learning progresses, you reinforce a smaller and smaller percentage of correct answers. This is called *intermittent reinforcement.*

How soon after the response should the reinforcer be presented? Again, scientific studies have shown that learning progresses differently depending on how soon after the response the reinforcer is presented. For example, effects may be different if the reinforcer is presented an hour or a day later. A rule of thumb is to present the reinforcer immediately after the response when the student is first learning something new. CBI can tirelessly and quickly perform this important function, as often as a student responds. Then as learning progresses, the time gap can be increased.

In CBI, reinforcers are given for correct answers, but reinforcers should also be given for student attention and participation. *Reinforcing participation* might take the form of a worded message such as "You're almost to your goal" or "Just five more problems to go." As with reinforcers for correct answers, musical tones or colors could also be used. Such messages could appear sprinkled throughout the lesson, or could be combined with the reinforcers given for correct answers. Remember, the reinforcer strengthens the response it follows and makes it more likely that the response (participating or answering correctly) will recur.

Table 6.2 presents a possible sequence of events which includes reinforcers both for participating and for answering correctly. Notice that consequent events can also function as antecedent events. This causes the instructional process to flow; it is not made up of discrete steps.

The second type of consequent event is a *punisher*. A punisher is a stimulus presented after a response which decreases the likelihood that the response will occur again. Punishing consequences stop things from happening again. (Many people do not like to use the word "punisher." If you would rather, think of punishers as decreasers.) Punishers help teach correct from incorrect. If the student makes an error, "knowledge of results" informing the student that an error has been made can be an effective punisher. Receiving information about errors made usually helps learning progress quickly.

In CBI, a punisher is used to tell the student that an error has been made and to decrease the likelihood that the error will recur. Punishing consequences take on a large number of forms and range from very mild (e.g., "Please try again) to very strong and objectionable (e.g., "Stupid answer").

Sometimes what we think will be a punisher turns out to be a reinforcer. An example of this in CBI could be an unattractive

TABLE 6.2 Sequence of Frames that Reinforce Participation as Well as Correct Response

Frame Number	Antecedent Event	Response	Consequent Event
1	Direction to read text on the next few frames	Attention Request next frame	Next frame
2.	Text	Attention Request next frame	Next frame
3.	Text	Attention Request next frame	Next frame, starts with "Only one more frame before you practice" to reinforce attention and participation so far
4.	Text plus direction to answer the practice question	Correct answer	"Correct" used to reinforce correct answer

graphic figure that develops with every error. If to complete the figure, the student has to make several errors, he or she is likely to try it. Similarly, students might try to make errors in order to hear ominous musical tones.

Only very mild punishers should be used in CBI. Courseware should be designed so that sustained struggling with the material does not occur. Too severe punishers can be demoralizing. They can also cause a student to avoid computers or even coursework completely. If too many punishers and too few reinforcers occur, the student may be left not doing anything—or left looking hard for his or her own reinforcers. Daydreaming, doodling, and talking are great escapes, for children and adults, if the instructional sequence is overly punishing.

There are four techniques to decrease the likelihood of errors in CBI. They are:

- Present mild, simple, tactful messages, tones, or graphics.
- Tell the student "incorrect" and give information that will help improve the next try.
- Response cost.
- Program natural punishers where possible.

Mild messages, tones, or graphics should be simple and tactful. A mild message might be "Please try again" or "Sorry, incorrect." A message saying only "Error" or "Wrong" is too harsh for many students. Even the word "No" presented time and time again can be frustrating. A single, perhaps low-pitched tone might be used as a mild punisher. A simple graphic symbol such as "?" or "X" or a patch of red could be presented on a screen with a student error. Regardless, encouragement to continue should be given at the same time.

Providing hints based on a computer assessment of the type of error increases the intelligence of the feedback. Meaningful information in CBI feedback makes the computer seem more human. Good human and computer instructors respond to incorrect answers with kindness, often a hint, and a second try.

One type of punisher, *response cost*, might be used in CBI, particularly in an instructional game. Response cost involves taking away a positive reinforcer that has previously been received if an error is made. Fining points or moving back spaces on a game board are examples of response-cost procedures.

Finally, a natural punisher is the obvious result of making an error. For example, if the pilot makes an error during training in a computerized flight simulator, the crashing plane is a natural punisher. No more words are necessary.

Shaping with Interactions

An interaction may be contained on one frame, or instructional text may be presented on frames preceding the query. (The pros and cons of displaying text with the query were discussed in Chapter 4.) The interaction query frame at least poses a question, may present a section of answers from which the student may choose, requires the student to respond, has space for student answer, and has space where feedback is presented.

Two important variables in the design of the interaction frame are combined to create interaction frames that shape a variety of responses. These variables are:

• The presence or absence of text during the query.
• The use of multiple-choice versus user-constructed responses.

By manipulating these variables, interactions are designed to teach mimic/copy skills, labeling and defining skills, and generalization skills.

The illustrations in this section show how changes in the antecedent event influence response shaping. The frames in Figures 6.2 and 6.3 present two interaction frames which teach a copy skill concerning the definition of the concept *modus ponens reasoning.* Both queries require the student to answer with some of the exact words that appear in the text portion of the frame. Figure 6.2 contains a three-choice multiple-choice answer, and Figure 6.3 requires the student to fill in a blank with a user-constructed answer. Figures 6.2 and 6.3 differ very little in the skills shaped because the correct answer is readily available on the text portion of the frame. The skill shaped by both frames is identity matching, and either answer mode accomplishes this. For copy skills, multiple-choice and user-constructed interactions shape similar skills.

What happens to the shaping potential of the same two frames if the text is not displayed during the interaction? Figures 6.4 and 6.5 illustrate. (Notice that the frame's functional area for the query remains constant even when the text functional area is empty.) First, the task in Figures 6.4 and 6.5 is more difficult than in Figures 6.2 and 6.3. Figures 6.4 and 6.5 could be considered interactions for copy skills even though the sample is not present, because the exact words used in the text are required in the student's response. Nevertheless, with text absent, the instructional objective

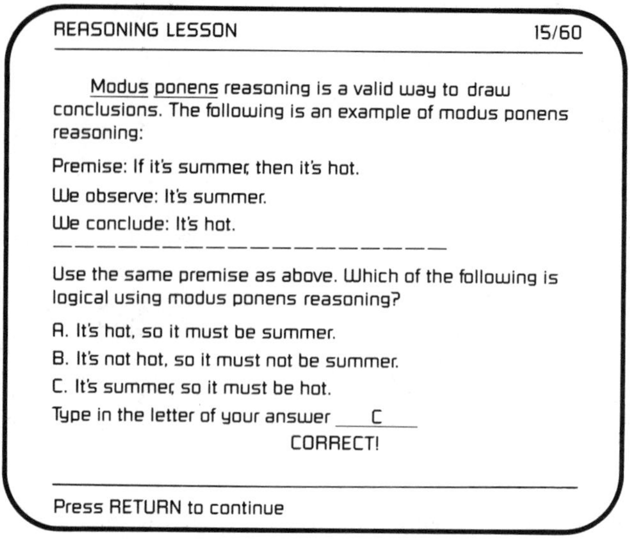

```
REASONING LESSON                                    15/60
─────────────────────────────────────────────────

     Modus ponens reasoning is a valid way to draw
conclusions. The following is an example of modus ponens
reasoning:

Premise: If it's summer, then it's hot.

We observe: It's summer.

We conclude: It's hot.
─ ─ ─ ─ ─ ─ ─ ─ ─ ─ ─ ─ ─ ─ ─ ─ ─ ─ ─ ─

Use the same premise as above. Which of the following is
logical using modus ponens reasoning?

A. It's hot, so it must be summer.

B. It's not hot, so it must not be summer.

C. It's summer, so it must be hot.

Type in the letter of your answer ___C___
                              CORRECT!

─────────────────────────────────────────────────

Press RETURN to continue
```

Figure 6-2. Interaction frame, text present, multiple choices given, to shape a copy skill.

```
REASONING LESSON                                    16/60
─────────────────────────────────────────────────

     Modus ponens reasoning is a valid way to draw
conclusions. The following is an example of modus ponens
reasoning:

Premise: If it's summer, then it's hot.

We observe: It's summer

We conclude: It's hot

─ ─ ─ ─ ─ ─ ─ ─ ─ ─ ─ ─ ─ ─ ─ ─ ─ ─

Use the same premise as above. If we observe that it's
summer, what do we conclude?

Type in your answer___It's very hot___
              CORRECT!

─────────────────────────────────────────────────

Press RETURN to continue
```

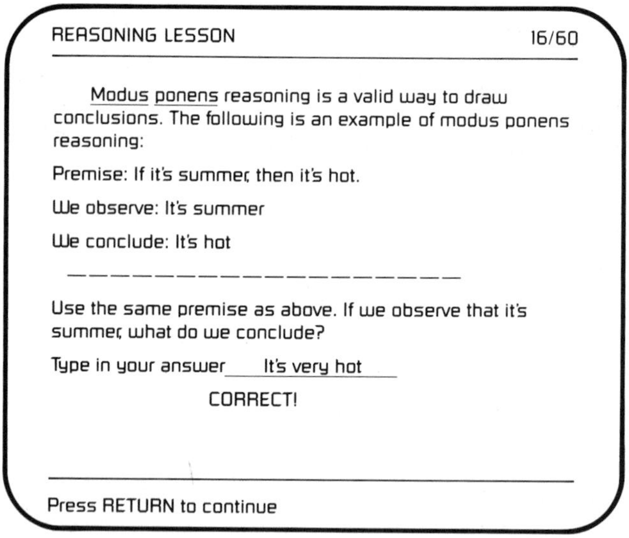

Figure 6-3. Interaction frame, text present, no answer choices given, to shape a copy skill.

```
╭─────────────────────────────────────────────────────╮
│  REASONING LESSON                          15/60      │
│  ─────────────────────────────────────────────       │
│                                                       │
│                                                       │
│     — — — — — — — — — — — — — —                       │
│                                                       │
│     The premise is: If it's summer, then it's hot. Which of the │
│     following is logical using modus ponens reasoning?│
│                                                       │
│     A. It's hot, so it must be summer.                │
│     B. It's not hot, so it must not be summer.        │
│     C. It's summer, so it must be hot.                │
│     Type in your answer _____C_____             │
│                            Correct. Good work.        │
│     ──────────────────────────────────────────       │
│  Press RETURN for next frame.                         │
╰─────────────────────────────────────────────────────╯
```

Figure 6-4. Interaction frame, text absent, answer choices given, to shape a difficult copy skill.

```
╭─────────────────────────────────────────────────────╮
│  REASONING LESSON                          17/60      │
│  ─────────────────────────────────────────────       │
│                                                       │
│                                                       │
│     — — — — — — — — — — — — — —                       │
│                                                       │
│     The premise is: If it's summer, then it's hot. We observe that │
│     it's summer. Using modus ponens reasoning, what can you │
│     conclude?                                         │
│     Type in your answer _____It's summer_____       │
│                      No. Please review the previous frame. │
│                                                       │
│                                                       │
│     ──────────────────────────────────────────       │
│  Press RETURN to continue, Press BACK to review       │
╰─────────────────────────────────────────────────────╯
```

Figure 6-5. Interaction frame, text absent, no answer choices given, to shape a difficult copy skill.

is more difficult than mere copying. A student must now generate an example of modus ponens, albeit an example that was just offered to the student. Either mode of answer entry (typing a "c" and typing "it must be hot") can accomplish the objective, as long as the computer has been programmed to accept typographical errors in the phrase answer.

In general, if text is presented on the interaction frame, a copy skill is shaped if the student is asked to select or produce an exact match of the text. However, a defining or labeling skill may be shaped with text present if the student is asked to select or produce a definition given a new example, or is asked to select or produce a new example of a previously learned definition. If text is not available during the interaction, the same range of instructional objectives is possible, except that memory of the initial presentation is now involved.

Meaningful Responses in Interactions

The student must be required to make meaningful responses as often as possible. For example, pressing the RETURN key to advance the frame is not meaningful in instruction, does not address instructional objectives, and does not count as an instructional interaction. In this same category falls overuse of multiple-choice items. Typing in single letters may be important in the early stages of identifying concepts and examples of concepts, but students must come to generate their own responses.

What the student is asked to do is what the student will learn to do. Examine the frames in Figure 6.6. Notice that in Figure 6.6A, the user copies the correct answer, present on the same frame, but in Figures 6.6B and C, the user actually constructs a response that is meaningful. The manner of behavior shaping exemplified in Figures 6.6B and C is more advanced than that used in Figure 6.6A. Notice also that a meaningful response can be produced using either a multiple-choice (Figure 6.6B) or user-constructed (Figure 6.6C) format.

Response Variety in Interactions

CBI accepts student input from many input devices. These include keyboard for typed responses; touchscreens that are sensitive to finger touch; joystick and mouse, which both allow quick, full-screen cursor movements and entering a response by pressing a button on the joystick or mouse; voice input, an input device under development which accepts spoken words; and eyescan, a new develop-

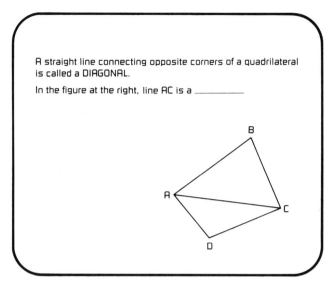

Figure 6-6A. A copy or "overcued" frame (from Cook, 1984).

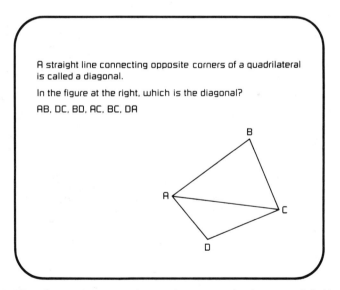

Figure 6-6B. Query that gets the student to apply the new definition.

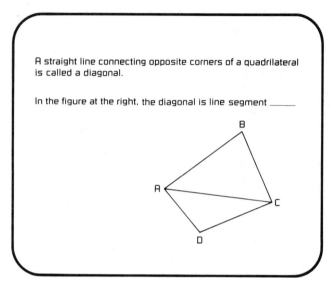

A straight line connecting opposite corners of a quadrilateral is called a diagonal.

In the figure at the right, the diagonal is line segment _____

Figure 6-6C. Query that gets the student to apply the new definition.

ment that accepts input from eyeblinks. No matter what input device is used, queries are worded to shape a variety of responses that are suggested by the instructional objectives.

Computers vary in the types of answers (such as multiple choice, user-constructed) they will accept, but a variety of skills can be shaped even with a limited capability system. For example, labeling a blank map of Sweden could be accomplished with a simple keyboard system by displaying on the screen a blank map with numbers at various locations, then having the student type in the city names, on lines with corresponding numbers. A mouse input device would permit students to type or write the names of the cities directly on the blank map on the computer screen.

Generally, computers accept short answers, but because of the wide range of computer capabilities, variety in test items is possible. These include: true–false, multiple-choice, matching, choosing opposites, fill in the blank with correct spelling, fill in the blank with any of several correct answers, activating action (such as movement in a particular direction, or changes in status of a situation), creating graphs, and coloring. Short-answer items may be written for all the performance levels and at all levels of difficulty. Short answers do not necessarily mean easy answers. Multiple-choice items can be written which require the student to draw inferences or solve problems.

Care must be taken, however, that long-answer items are not excluded from the curriculum. Long answers can be handled by a

CBI system that accepts only short answers if the long answer is obtained through a series of short-answer questions. For example, the question "Describe the sequence of events involved in performing a chemical titration" requires a long answer. The answer can be obtained by asking "What is the first step in performing a chemical titration?" then "What is the second step?" and so on. If such a technique proves unwieldy, long-answer items should simply be administered in some way other than CBI. For example, if a long answer is required, the program could stop, the student would write the answer on paper or type it into the computer, then call the teacher to have the answer judged (Chase, 1985). The teacher would then recommend new material or review, based on the student's answer.

Determining the Number of Interactions Needed

CBI designers need information about the desired ratio of text frames to interaction frames. One study compared the differences in performance produced by different ratios of text to interaction frames (Schloss, Schloss, & Cartwright, 1984). Four conditions were compared: 90:1 (no interactions), 5:1, 3:1, and 1:1 (an interaction on every frame). The lowest performance scores were associated with the lesson containing no interactions. There were no differences in performance as a function of the other three ratios, but the differences in these ratios is not extreme.

Another interesting aspect of this study was its comparison of the use of interaction/query frames versus simple review/restatement frames with no queries. Better performance was associated with lessons containing interactions as opposed to lessons that contained only review frames. However, student opinion was favorable toward frequent use of the review frames. Student opinion was especially negative toward the format of an interaction on every frame. The authors suggest that a mix of interaction and review frames is appropriate. They also suggest that designers take care to program only nontrivial interactions so as not to anger students who rightly perceive that trivial interactions are a waste of time.

A related study compared the effects of use of questions versus use of review statements and use of factual versus generalization items, using three ratios (Schloss, Sindelar, Cartright, & Schloss, 1986). The ratios used were 45:15 questions to review statements, 30:30, and 15:45. Student performance was better on sequences using more questions than on review statements. The mix of factual and generalization questions did not affect final exam scores, but subjects preferred the sequences with more factual than generalization questions. The authors speculate that the relatively unhelpful feedback for errors, "Incorrect, select another answer," may have been frustrating to students who missed generalization questions.

Rightly assuming that interactions should be frequent in CBI, one corporation has provided a positive contingency for the CBI designer's behavior of scheduling frequent interactions. CBI designers' performance is measured in hours of CBI produced. The corporation has functionally defined "an hour of CBI" as 60 interactions. This contingency encourages designers to program frequent interactions and decreases the number of text frames without interactions. Of course, trivial interactions should be excluded from the count.

Remedial Frames

Remedial frames increase the instructional power of CBI because they individualize instruction. A distinction may be drawn between self-paced and individualized instruction. In self-paced instruction, the student controls the speed of instruction, as is the case with CBI, but traditional nonadaptive instruction may also be self-paced. Standard textbooks may be used in self-paced courses. In individualized instruction, instructional presentations are tailored to the performance of the student. CBI without adaptive presentations wastes one of the most valuable instructional features of CBI. Thus, designing remedial frames is an important part of courseware design.

Remedial frames provide feedback based on the student's response on a single frame and based on the student's pattern of errors. Most CBI provides feedback based on single responses. More intelligent courseware provides feedback based on error patterns, but very little has been written about remedial strategies for incorrect response patterns.

Remedial Frames for Single Errors

CBI presents remedial frames for the first two or three errors but does not allow a student to give an incorrect answer over and over without interfering. CBI should prevent a student from receiving reinforcement for a lucky guess or an answer given because it was the only one not yet tried on a fourth or fifth try. A student should be given only one try on a two-choice multiple-choice question.

CBI can either have the student try again, without providing the correct answer, or it can provide the correct answer and either repeat the same question or branch to another sequence. Options for remedial frames are described below.

1. Ask the student to try again without providing the correct answer.

- Retain the same instructional objective and repeat the interaction (query) over again. This remedial frame is usually presented on a first error.
- Retain the same instructional objective and repeat the interaction (text and query) over again. This is a frame choice for a first error.
- Retain the same instructional objective and present a hint based on the student's error. This is a frame choice for a first or second error.

2. Provide the correct answer and repeat the same sequence or branch to a simpler sequence.

- Tell the student the correct answer and present the same query over again. This is a frame choice for a first, second, or third error.
- Tell the student the correct answer, retain the same instructional objective, but branch the student to a sequence of frames with the same material broken into smaller and simpler steps. This is a frame choice for a second or third error.
- Tell the student the correct answer, abandon the instructional objective, and branch the student to a sequence of frames which introduces or reviews a requisite skill. This is a frame choice for a second or third error.

There are no rules for when to use which remedial frames. For a first error, re-presentation of the same question sometimes suffices. For a first or second error, a hint is usually in order. For a third error, the entire sequence or an alternative sequence, not just the query, should be re-presented.

As a system increases in intelligence, hints become more tailored to the student's responses. The feedback "Incorrect, please try again" shows only the grossest level of sensitivity, because this one error message can be used for any incorrect answer.

The next step up in sensitivity is a system that provides a special error message for every error choice. For a multiple-choice query, the designer writes a special message for every foil. For example, if the query is "What is the capital of Italy" and the student selects "Paris," a tailored message would be "Incorrect. Paris is the capital of France. Please try again." For another example, if the query requires the correct answer "tortuous" and the student selects "torturous," the feedback could be "Torturous refers to painful ordeals, not to winding roads."

Another step up in sensitivity is a system using fill-in-the-blank questions that does not require exact matches. In this case, using the same question above, if the student types in "Roam," the feedback message could be "Correct, but you misspelled it. ROME is the capital of Italy."

Remedial Frames for Error Patterns

Few CBI systems diagnose student error patterns and provide help based on the pattern. This is the type of thing that good human teachers do well: They ask a student several questions until they determine what misconceptions the student holds. Then they tell the student what the problem appears to be; for example, "You seem to be forgetting that warm air rises." Sometimes a student says "Oh, NOW I get it" when given information specially tailored to fit his or her unique pattern of answers. The teacher is not operating on a formula but using judgment based on knowledge of the topic under study.

Intelligence in diagnosing error patterns and providing specially tailored help is new to CBI. There is no research comparing methods of determining faulty patterns or determining methods of providing help for a particular pattern. This area of endeavor is challenging and will be a topic of great interest in CBI into the 1990s.

One intelligent CBI system called "Recovery Boiler Tutor" diagnoses two error patterns (Woolf & McDonald, 1984). The Recovery Boiler Tutor provides reinforced simulation practice in management of huge recovery boilers in the paper industry. It determines if the student consistently fails to draw conclusions or if the student makes errors that do not fall into that pattern. The system leads the student to synthesize information if the former pattern is determined, or redirects the student if the second condition is determined.

A great deal of effort has been invested in determining faulty error patterns in the responses of children learning elementary subtraction (Burton, 1982). This system, called "Buggy," is one of the best known intelligent CBI systems. Approximately 110 simple error patterns or "bugs" have been identified; if these simple patterns are combined, 100,000,000 bugs result. The simple bugs in clude "$0 - n = n$," "$n - 0 = 0$, "smaller from larger," and "stop working on a problem when the bottom number runs out."

Review Frames

Reviews are summaries of previously learned material. They do not require a student response in the same way that practice and tests do. Reviews are an important part of introducing new material; for example, as stage setters. Reviews are also used to prepare a student for a test. Good scheduling of reviews is an important component of instruction.

Review is especially important in CBI, perhaps more so in CBI than in textbook instruction. Several factors are involved. First, the student cannot freely page back in CBI, and long-term memory demands are thus increased in CBI. Second, to complicate matters, less information is presented per CBI frame than is presented per textbook page, so less information is readily available in the field of vision. Short-term memory is taxed. Third, much CBI relies on auxiliary sources such as printed handbooks or oral information provided by the teacher. Important review may be difficult to obtain from a handbook while the student's attention is focused on the computer screen, and the review information should thus be presented on the screen. CBI review serves the important function it performs in all instructional media, but also plays a special role in CBI.

Review of previously learned material appears before the introduction of a new point. Reviews in introductions provide context for the new material and make the new material more meaningful. Review of current instructional points occurs just prior to unit testing. This review either repeats in summary what was taught or ties together all the points. Review before testing is often associated with higher test scores than if review is omitted.

The importance of review is illustrated in work by Collins (1974). In a series of three experiments, Collins compared variants of methods of sequencing in CBI. One method was based on sequences used by expert teachers. These teachers first asked questions to determine what students already knew about the new topic. Then they related a bit of new information to that already known even if the old information had been learned in a previous lesson (*across block*). Thus depth of review was a component of good teaching.

The teachers repeated the sequence over and over until the topic had been mastered at the required level of depth. Students were allowed to ask questions during instruction. This approach is called *web teaching*, where old information is interlocked with new.

The second method also began instruction taking off from information already learned. Students answered questions but could not ask them. New material was related only to previously learned information *within block*. Review depth was thus shallow. The studies found that across block or in-depth review was superior to within-block review in introducing new material.

The frames in Figure 6.7 illustrate a review before a test. A review need not be confined to one frame. A review briefly describes the lesson topic. The review also allows the student a chance to restudy the lesson or take the test.

CBI Tests

Purpose

Tests provide an opportunity for students to demonstrate their mastery of the instructional material, after reinforced practice with

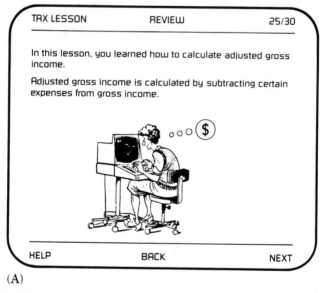

(A)

Figure 6-7. Review sequence before a lesson test.

```
┌─────────────────────────────────────────────────┐
│  TAX LESSON          REVIEW            26/30      │
│  ───────────────────────────────────────────     │
│  You also learned what expenses are allowed in the│
│  adjustment, and which expenses are not.          │
│  In general, allowable subtractions include:      │
│        • Business expenses                        │
│        • Job-related moving expenses              │
│        • Some charitable contributions            │
│        • Alimony                                  │
│                                                   │
│  ───────────────────────────────────────────     │
│  HELP              BACK               NEXT        │
└─────────────────────────────────────────────────┘
```

(B)

Figure 6-7. Continued.

```
┌─────────────────────────────────────────────────┐
│  TAX LESSON          REVIEW            27/30      │
│  ───────────────────────────────────────────     │
│  Your test on this lesson will ask you to:        │
│        • Determine allowable and non-allowable subtractions│
│        • Calculate adjusted gross income          │
│                                                   │
│  Please review the lesson if you are not ready for the test.│
│  The test includes 10 items where you must determine if the│
│  expense is an allowable adjustment. You will also have to│
│  calculate an adjusted gross income. You will have 15 minutes│
│  to complete the test.                            │
│                                                   │
│  ───────────────────────────────────────────     │
│  HELP              REVIEW             TEST        │
└─────────────────────────────────────────────────┘
```

(C)

Figure 6-7. Continued.

interactions. Practice interactions appear frequently during instruction, and tests are administered less frequently. Test scores reflect the quality of the CBI, and to a lesser extent, reflect student effort in completing the interactions and preparing for the test.

As described in Chapter 3, well-written instructional objectives suggest test items. Test items ask about material covered in the previous lesson or unit of lessons. The test gives the student a fair chance at demonstrating skill.

Test items measure the skills actually taught. For example, the test on an introductory CBI lesson covering the geography of Sweden might ask a student to label cities on a blank map of Sweden, but would not include identifying key government officials in Sweden. Depending on lesson content and objectives, the student could be asked to label the map given a list of cities, or the student could be asked to generate the names without referring to a list. Instructional objectives of the lesson cover goals of the lesson, interactions are keyed to objectives, and test questions concern interactions. Tests contain items identical or similar to practice items, especially

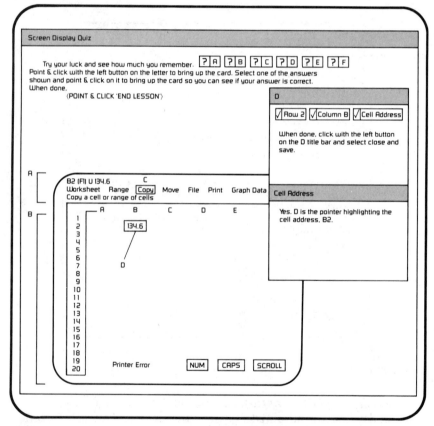

Figure 6-8. Quiz problem from CBI to teach LOTUS 1-2-3 (courtesy of Joseph Psotka, U.S. Army Research Institute).

tests of acquisition and fluency. Test items on proficiency maintenance and generalization vary considerably from practice interactions.

Figure 6.8 presents a test item from a CBI module which teaches LOTUS 1-2-3. This test item asks the student to identify the location of the number indicated by the D. The student correctly identified the location as "row 2, column b," and the system provided correct feedback in the "cell address" window.

Figure 6.9 presents an example of a paper test (printed in the student handbook) used within the U.S. Senate's CBI lesson to teach word processing. (The screen format for the lesson was presented in Figure 4.3). Using a paper test mimics "real life" where a word-processing employee would be given back his or her letter with corrections marked. Then the employee must make the required changes. In the case of Figure 6.9, the student retrieves the original letter, makes the five required changes in the computer, and refiles the document using the same name.

CBI tests should be reliable and valid. Reliability refers to test score consistency across repeated administrations. Validity refers to the degree to which the items test the required topics. These two concepts are described below.

Reliability

A test is reliable if a test taker receives nearly the same scores on multiple administrations of the same or highly similar tests. Test reliability is assessed by readministering the same test, dividing the test in halves and administering each half separately, or constructing equivalent forms of the test and administering them. Many computers have the capability of constructing multiple forms of the same test by drawing items randomly from an item pool.

Reliability is important in CBI tests because only with reliable tests can changes in student scores from pretest to posttest be determined. Using an unreliable test to measure student performance is like using a rubber ruler to measure the length of an object; variations in measures will result, but the variations will have nothing to do with actual variations in the real state of the ruler.

There are several ways to increase the reliability of a test. First, all test questions must be clearly worded. Vague instructions and wording will decrease reliability, because student guessing increases. Guessing increases error from one test admininstration to the next. Second, multiple forms of the same test must have roughly the same number of questions at each difficulty level tested. This implies that the test item pool should contain items of each difficulty

February 21, 1986

Mr. Joaquin Padillo ∧, *President* ①
Padillo Waste Management ∧, *Inc.* ②
41 Ash Street, SW
Miami, FL 32201

Dear Mr. Padillo,

③ thank you for sending me the article from the Miami Tribune on waste management in South Florida. I am aware of ~~some of the~~ problems ④ ⑤ companies in your business face.

I have asked my aide, Don Jackson, to keep you informed about federal legislation on solid waste environmental issues.

Please feel free to let me know your views in the future.

Sincerely,

Thomas B. Jones
United States Senate

✗ = remove
∧ = insert
≡ = capitalize

3. REFILE THIS DOCUMENT WITH THE SAME NAME

Figure 6-9. Paper test incorporated into CBI lesson to teach word processing (courtesy of Training Section, U.S. Senate Computer Center).

level, proportional to the instructional objectives under study. For example, if generalization is the thrust of the lesson, the test item pool should contain more generalization items than items at other levels of difficulty. Thus when items are drawn from the pool to construct alternate forms, it will be likely that more generalization items than simpler items will end up in the new test, thus increasing test reliability. Third, longer tests are usually more reliable than short tests. This is because longer tests provide a more complete picture of the student's level.

To determine test–retest or alternate-form reliability, several students are administered the test, or alternate forms of the test, twice within a two-week period. If the test is reliable, the average group scores should be close from test 1 to test 2, providing of course that the students do not receive instruction in the interim.

Test reliability may also be estimated by using one student's score for one test administration (called split-half reliability). In this method, the student's score on half the items (say the even-numbered items) is compared to the score on the other half of the items. If the test is reliable, the student's scores will be nearly the same for both halves.

Many CBI test designers are interested in statistical reliability estimates such as those described above. If the test is one that will frequently be used, as is the case with many CBI tests because they are so easily administered to multiple students, reliability quotients are important. They indicate how well the items are written and keyed to the instruction. If a student scores high on one test and low on a supposedly equivalent form, both sets of items should be examined to determine which need rewording or excluding. [For more information, the reader should consult Anastasi (1988).]

Validity

Test validity is a broad concept, and three types of validity are important in CBI tests: face, content, and criterion validity. When discussing test validity, one always specifies the type of validity. Face and content validity are routine concerns of CBI designers. Criterion validity is examined less often.

Face validity refers to the appearance of the test items: Do the items look like they test the proper subject matter? Although face validity may seem at first glance to be a trivial concern, it is important to test users and test takers who react initially to the test by looking to see if the test "looks" fair. Face validity is judged informally by one or more experts who decide if the test is face valid. The test writer is often too close to the test to be able to make a fair assessment about face validity.

Content validity refers to how well the test items cover the desired content and the extent to which the student's answers are influenced by the shaping that took place in the CBI lesson, as opposed to extraneous factors. It is very important that the test writer or test user assess content validity. When writing test items, the test writer should list all teaching points (e.g., concepts, concept components, task, and subtasks) covered, and the proportion of instruction or the number of interactions spent on each point. The number of test items per content point should be proportional to the number of practice interactions per content point. If two practice interactions covered basic definitions and 10 practice interactions covered generalization items, the ratio of basic definition to generalization test items should be 1:5.

Careful item writing is required to assure that the student's answers are influenced by knowledge gained in the lesson as opposed to extraneous factors, such as poorly written test items. Often, CBI test items are answered with short answers; sometimes several correct answers (such as synonyms or misspellings) are acceptable, but sometimes not. It is difficult to write one- or two-sentence questions that are free of ambiguity, so it is desirable to try out new items on a colleague before using them in a test.

Criterion validity refers to how well one test predicts performance on another test or in a "real-life" situation. Criterion validity is important when the test results are used to make predictions past the present CBI lesson. (Face and content validity do not make predicitions about how the student will perform on other tests or in the future.) Criterion validity is important in simulation testing, where it is expected that the student's performance in the simulation is indicative of performance in real life.

Statistical procedures, instead of expert colleague judgments, generate indexes of criterion validity. These procedures correlate a student's score on the test to scores on other tests (the criterion measures). Criterion validity is important with widely used standardized tests such as the Scholastic Aptitude Test, or SAT. Criterion validity research with the SAT correlates scores on the SAT with grades in college to determine if the SAT scores are useful in predicting success.

Criterion validity is also important in government, business, and industry. These agencies and organizations find that it is less expensive to administer a good predictive test than to take a chance on someone and provide a tryout in a real-life situation. People who do not pass the simulation tests are not placed in real-life situations. (A notable example of this is with pilot certification in the airline industry.) Therefore, simulation tests in these settings must demonstrate good predictive or criterion validity.

Study Questions

Definition Questions

1. What are some characteristics of a good introduction?
2. What are the similarities and differences between behavior shaping and generalization?
3. What is a meaningful interaction?
4. What remedial work should a student get for the first error? second error? third error? subsequent errors, if any?
5. What are some characteristics of a good review?
6. Give three reasons why review is particularly important in CBI.
7. Define *test reliability*. How is reliability measured?
8. Define *test validity*. How is validity measured?

Discussion Questions

1. Describe the behavior-shaping process that occurs within an interaction sequence.
2. What is the difference in student performance produced by queries presented with text present versus queries with text absent?
3. Which is more difficult for students—multiple choice or fill in the blanks where no answer choices are given? Justify your answer.
4. What is the best ratio of text frames to queries? the worst ratio? Explain.
5. Describe how one increases CBI sensitivity with respect to error analysis.
6. What might some error patterns be with students answering the study questions at the end of the chapters in this book?
7. Is it better to use review questions or review statements? Explain.
8. How do you make a CBI test reliable?
9. How do you make a CBI test valid?

CHAPTER 7

Tailoring CBI Interactions for Specific Performance Levels

The main topics in this chapter are:

- *Interactions for acquisition performance level*
- *Interactions for fluency building*
- *Interactions for generalization*
- *Interactions for proficiency maintenance*

Introduction

Students display a characteristic performance when they are first introduced to a new idea. The performance is weak, errors are made, answers or actions come slowly. However, with time spent in instruction, the same student who once struggled with a new concept comes to master it and eventually may learn to use the concept in solving difficult problems.

Levels in student performance reflect levels of learning. The performance levels are not necessarily clear-cut and distinct, and every learner may not attain each level for each skill in the curriculum. However, recognizing differences in types of performance helps us select CBI procedures. The levels are: acquisition, fluency building, generalization, and proficiency maintenance. These are illustrated in Figure 7.1.

Chapter 6 described how to write introduction, interaction, remedial, review, and test frames for any courseware sequence. In this chapter, CBI techniques for tailoring interactions for each performance level are described. The focus of this chapter is changes in interactions as a function of performance level.

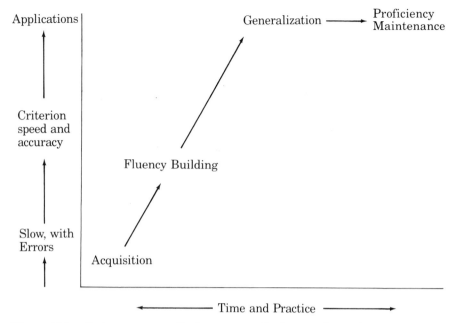

Figure 7.1. Performance quality increases with time and practice.

CBI Techniques for Acquisition

Design of Acquisition-Level Sequences

An *acquisition-level* performance is slow, imperfect, or off-target. This is an entry-level performance. The student needs special attention from the courseware to make clear what performance is correct and to encourage the student to continue trying. Shaping techniques, involving clear explicit antecedent material and response consequences, are used to improve the quality of weak, beginner-level responses.

Antecedent material must be clearly worded for acquisition-level performing. The first presentation of a new fact, idea, or task is clearly stated. In acquisition, it is good to present only a small amount of information per frame, or allow the student to add information to the frame by pressing a key. It is helpful to isolate the new bit of information. This is accomplished by highlighting. Once a new fact is clearly presented, the query sets up the learner to give one simple response. The frames in Figure 7.2 show clearly

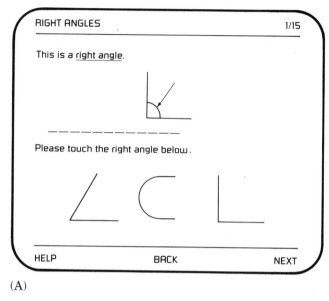

Figure 7.2. Antecedent events and queries in acquisition sequences.

presented material and a direct, unambiguous query related to the material.

The design of consequent events is important for teaching acquisition-level performance. It is important that feedback (a reinforcer or a punisher, as you will recall from Chapter 6) be provided after *every* response made during acquisition. A student learning a new skill or fact needs the information provided by feedback. It is also important that the feedback be provided soon after the response is made; long delays stifle motivation and cause the student to lose attention. The consequence should be simple and clear.

Wording is important when designing feedback for acquisition-level performances. Usually, a mildly worded and short-feedback message such as "Correct" or "Yes" is sufficient. It is important that the student be able to tell immediately if the answer has been judged correct or not. A feedback message such as "That's what I would have said" could mean correct or incorrect. "Correct, nice work" represents a medium amount of reinforcing feedback, and feedback such as "Wow!! You're the greatest!!!" is a large amount. Unkind or curt feedback such as "Finally you have gotten it right" is to be avoided completely, and exaggerated feedback with long messages, tones, and flashers is usually unnecessary.

It is advisable to vary the feedback message. Sometimes the message includes a restatement of the correct answer such as "Correct.

PLURALISM   1/15

A <u>pluralist</u> society gives importance to many views. A democracy is a pluralist society. A communistic society is not pluralist.

————————————————————

A democracy is a ___pluralist___ society because it gives importance to many views.

HELP   BACK   NEXT

(B)

Figure 7.2. Continued.

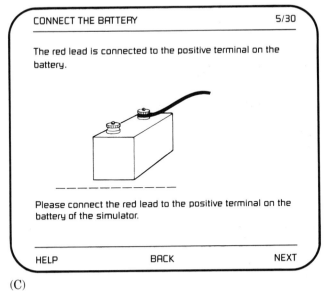

CONNECT THE BATTERY   5/30

The red lead is connected to the positive terminal on the battery.

————————————————

Please connect the red lead to the positive terminal on the battery of the simulator.

HELP   BACK   NEXT

(C)

Figure 7.2. Continued.

Paris is the capital of France." It is not necessary to restate every correct answer, however. Some authoring systems randomly select messages from a pool of messages. At the same time, care must be taken that feedback messages are not so variable that the student must slow down to read them.

In acquisition, there are two situations in which a large amount of reinforcement might be appropriate; both are related to increasing motivation. One, if the student needs extra motivation, for example, if the student is a child, exaggerated reinforcement may hold attention. Two, exaggerated reinforcement may bring a smile to the face of a teenaged or adult student if it is presented only occasionally. If exaggerated reinforcement is overused, however, it loses its novelty and surprise effects, and may even become annoying. Exaggerated reinforcement takes longer to present than a small amount of reinforcement, and if overused will lengthen training time unnecessarily.

If musical tones, voices, or flashers are available on the computer, a single pleasant tone (one note) represents a small amount, a short tune (about five notes) is a medium amount, and songs, whistles, and flashers combined represent a large amount of reinforcement.

The message "Please try again" represents a small amount of corrective feedback; "No, your answer is incorrect" is a greater measure of corrective feedback; and a message such as "Wrong!!! Are you asleep???" is a large amount of unkind feedback and is never appropriate. In acquisition, a small amount of corrective feedback is required and the correct answer is usually given such as "No. PARIS is the capital of France," and the query is repeated.

Introducing Examples and Nonexamples

As soon as the query is correctly answered, the next bit of information is presented. To learn a concept, the student must be able to select and generate examples and nonexamples of the concept as well as learn to label examples correctly with the concept name. After a query about an example has been answered correctly, an example or nonexample is then introduced.

Guidance about teaching concepts is offered by Englemann and Carnine (1982). (Their book is a rich source of detailed information about concept teaching, although the book is not written for CBI design; interested readers should consult that text.) More than one example of the concept must be presented. The examples chosen should illustrate the range of characteristics found in examples of the concept. Third, negative examples of the concept should have something in common with examples. This helps the student iden-

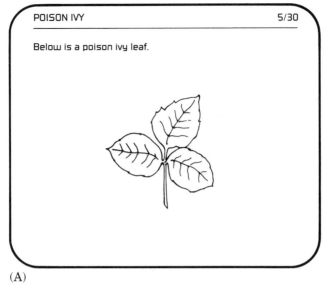

POISON IVY   5/30

Below is a poison ivy leaf.

(A)

Figure 7.3. Acquisition-level sequence in concept teaching. (Figure 7.3B–F continued on pp. 166 to 168.)

tify noncritical characteristics of the concept. Finally, a negative example that appears only minimally different from the positive example teaches sharp discriminations between examples and non-examples. These difficult discriminations are introduced after easier discriminations have been mastered.

The frames in Figure 7.3 present a sample portion from a CBI sequence which might be used to teach the concept of *poison ivy leaf*. Notice that examples and a nonexample are introduced. After only a few frames of text, the student is asked to demonstrate acquisition by answering first a simple question, then a more difficult question. The responses called for are meaningful in the sequence.

Many CBI systems vary the number of examples and nonex-amples presented to the student based on a mastery requirement. Designers construct a pool of example and nonexample queries, and the computer draws from the pool until the student meets an accuracy requirement.

Techniques for Building Fluency

Once a student begins to perform more quickly and with greater accuracy, the student is ready to continue to improve, so the per-

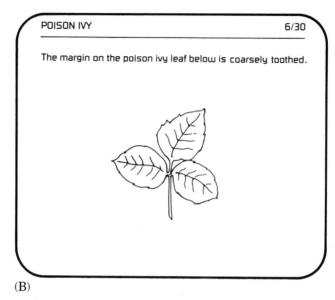

(B)

Figure 7.3. Continued.

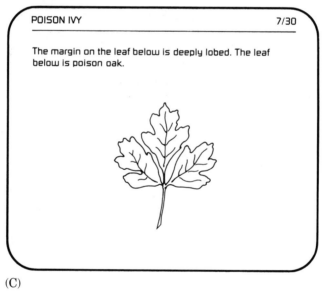

(C)

Figure 7.3. Continued.

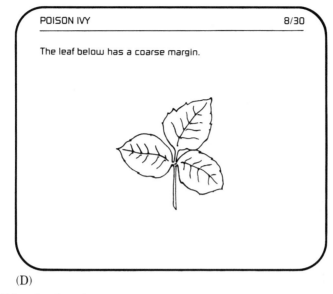

(D)

Figure 7.3. Continued.

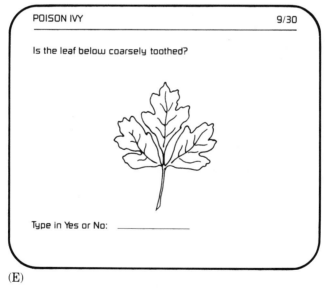

(E)

Figure 7.3. Continued.

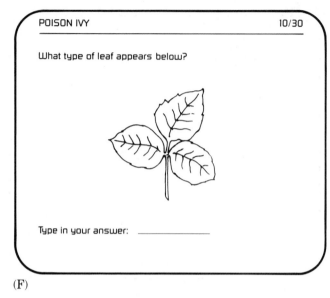

(F)

Figure 7.3. Continued.

formance becomes more useful and more correct. İt may be that answering questions or performing a task more quickly, more accurately, or both is desirable. During *fluency building*, the interactions in the courseware change to help the student refine the performance. The goal of fluency building is to bring performance up to a useful level. Changes in the antecedent events are called for in the shaping plan for this level. No longer is it necessary to give explicit prompts and directions. Less information can be used in the directions.

The goal of fluency building is to improve an acquisition-level performance into a usable skill. Teaching techniques for fluency building are associated with increasing two aspects of the performance: accuracy and speed. The technique used most often at this level is drill with feedback. The antecedent material in drill is simple and repetitive (White & Haring, 1976).

Drill need not be boring! As mentioned earlier, the goal of fluency building is to master exactly (or nearly exactly) what was previously introduced. It is not the goal of fluency drill to teach or require imaginative answers. Nonetheless, fluency-building drills in imaginative contexts can increase motivation and even pave the way for expanded use of the skill, which will come later.

During fluency building practice, feedback is provided frequently. The necessity of frequent feedback is due to the fact that the student enters this performance level from acquisition level, where performance may be accurate to some extent but is neither consistent nor quick. Drill for fluency building simply provides an opportunity for students to practice exactly what was introduced during acquisition.

Examples of drill formats include drill games and drill races that provide frequent feedback. One drill format was presented in Figure 1.2.

The frames in Figure 7.4 illustrate a drill race. Notice how the introductory frame encourages an increase in speed and accuracy. Notice that the goal of the drill is stated. Motivation is increased by displaying the student's cumulated score at the top of each frame during the game. During acquisition, the student had learned three chemicals and their smells: amyl acetate/banana, citral/lemon, and benzene/kerosene. Now the student needs to match the substance with its odor *and* to do it quickly. If the time criterion (10 correct in 1 minute) is met, we have a good indication that the correct answers are not just guesses. Notice that feedback is given after each answer. Also notice that even though the missed question is re-presented immediately, the format of the answer choices changes slightly.

(A)

Figure 7.4. Drill game format for fluency building. (Figure 7.4 B–D continued on pp. 170 and 171.)

```
GAME   Score: Round 1.   0 correct.
_____

Here is the chemical: AMYL ACETATE
What does it smell like? Touch your choice.
              Sour
              Banana
              Eggs
_ _ _ _ _ _ _ _ _ _ _ _ _ _

GOOD. Amyl acetate/Banana
_ _ _ _ _ _ _ _ _ _ _ _ _ _
```

(B)

Figure 7.4. Continued.

```
GAME   Score: Round 1, 1 Correct in 12 Seconds
_____

Here is the chemical: CITRAL
What does it smell like? Touch your choice.
              Cabbage
              Sweet
              Lemon
_ _ _ _ _ _ _ _ _ _ _ _ _ _

Nope, sorry. Citral/Lemon
_ _ _ _ _ _ _ _ _ _ _ _ _ _
```

(C)

Figure 7.4. Continued.

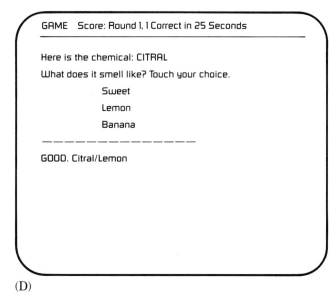

(D)

Figure 7.4. Continued.

Techniques for Generalization

Next, it is important for the student to be able to use the skill in new situations. In the new situations, the skill may be explicitly required, or the student may select to use the skill without being prompted. Examples of generalization include problem solving and creativity. Again, the interactions in the courseware must change to bring the student's performance to the level of generalization. Antecedent events at this level become more loosely structured and contain variety. Specially programmed reinforcers seldom need be delivered. Natural reinforcers occur often when students are solving problems and acting in creative ways.

Generalization is the process by which the student comes to use newly acquired skills in new situations without being taught to do so explicitly. Generalization describes the basic ways in which people learn and think. Generalization is involved in much of what we do, whether academic or not. Fostering generalization is important in instruction because when the student generalizes, time is saved and the student's confidence increases.

Three generalization processes have been identified: (1) physical generalization (called *primary stimulus generalization* or *abstraction* by researchers), (2) rule learning (or *recombinative generalization*), and (3) analogy learning (or *stimulus equivalence generalization*) (Spradlin, Karlan, & Wetherby, 1976). Knowing about the three types of generalization—physical generalization, rule learning, and analogy—tells a CBI designer that every aspect or example of a new concept does not have to be taught explicitly. Economical instruction carefully selects examples and nonexamples of a concept for explicit teaching to maximize the effects of generalization. The antecedent events that foster the three types of generalization are described below.

Generalization Based on Physical Similarity

Physical generalization is the process by which a student learns a response, then makes the same response again in a different situation. This type of generalization is caused by physical similarities between the first stimulus and the new stimuli. Stimulus generalization underlies learning to label, such as learning to call a variety of chairs *chair*. All chairs share certain physical similarities. This process is also involved in physical activities and accounts for the way people learn to ride their own bicycle and can also ride the bicycles of their friends. Generalization of this type is desirable, and CBI can be designed to increase generalization. This is done by presenting new stimulus material which is physically similar to material already introduced, and asking for a response without explicitly teaching the student how to respond to each stimulus.

The frame in Figure 7.5 depicts an exercise to teach generalization based on the physical similarity between the teaching example and the practice example. Use of this type of exercise results in instructional efficiency because the fact that right angles are right angles regardless of orientation does not have to be explicitly taught. In addition, students experience the positive feeling that comes from figuring out something new, seemingly without assistance.

Generalization Based on Rule Learning

Rule learning (or recombinative generalization) describes the process by which people explicitly learn a small number of responses, then come to combine the responses in new ways without being taught. This can create a multiplicative increase in new responses. For example, if a student learns to point correctly to a red ball, a red bat, and a green ball, the student will probably also be able to point to a green bat without having been taught this explicitly.

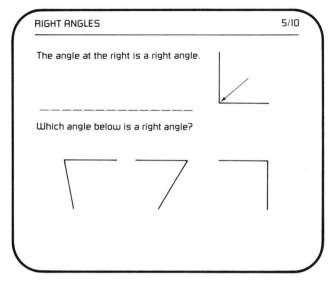

Figure 7.5. Exercise to foster primary stimulus generalization.

If a third color is then taught, the number of correct responses made without training increases again. The frame in Figure 7.6 depicts an exercise to teach generalization based on recombination.

Generalization Based on Analogy

Analogy learning (or stimulus equivalence generalization) works similar to physical generalization—a student learns a response, then makes the same response again in a new situation. The difference is that stimulus equivalence is not based on the physical similarities between stimuli, but is based on analogy. For example, the student may learn that the Soviet Union and Yugoslavia are communist countries, then learn that Soviets earn low wages and infer that Yugoslavs must also earn low wages. This is a basic process that we all experience. The logic may be faulty as well as accurate. However, when correct, CBI fosters efficiency in learning by allowing the student to learn by inference and analogy.

The frames in Figure 7.7 depict an exercise to teach generalization based on analogy between the teaching and practice examples. The student equates problems maintained by social attention with tantrums, nagging, and cursing, and does not have to be taught a treatment for each problem separately. If each problem is later discussed separately, the student will already have been exposed to the treatment through use of this exercise.

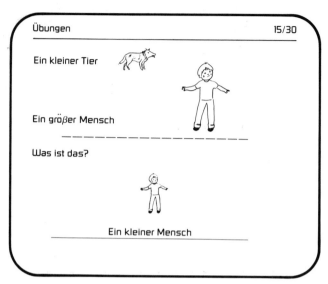

Figure 7.6. Exercise to foster recombinative generalization.

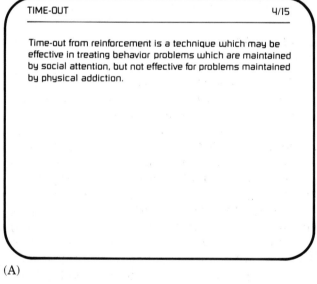

(A)

Figure 7.7. Exercise to foster generalization by stimulus equivalence or analogy.

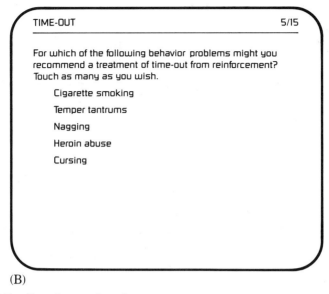

TIME-OUT   5/15

For which of the following behavior problems might you recommend a treatment of time-out from reinforcement? Touch as many as you wish.

    Cigarette smoking

    Temper tantrums

    Nagging

    Heroin abuse

    Cursing

(B)

Figure 7.7. Exercise continued.

Generalization Drill, Games, and Simulations

When teaching a student to generalize a skill, we can specifically teach the student to apply the skill to a new situation. We may also present the student with a problem whose solution may rest on application of the skill or concept, but we will not tell the student the relation between the skill and the solution. In either case, we are teaching problem solving or creativity.

There are three general techniques that are useful for teaching a student to apply a previously learned skill: (1) mixed practice drills, (2) advanced games, and (3) simulations of real-life situations.

Computer-based instruction is particularly well suited for these techniques because of the interesting variety of drills, games, and simulations that is possible on computers. Variety is important in teaching generalization. Figure 7.8 illustrates the use of a simulated situation in which the student has to apply previously learned information. In this sequence the student handles a lifelike situation with a client.

Mixed-practice drills, like the drills used to build fluency or maintain proficiency, allow for repeated practice. Mixed-practice drills, however, differ from drills that are confined to drilling previously learned material in only one context. A mixed-practice drill for teaching generalization of a simple skill, multiplying 4 times 2, might require the student to multiply 2 bags of oranges carried

CLIENT BACKGROUND

Paul Smith is a 48 year old Certified Public Accountant with a private practice. He earns about $65k, which places him in the highest tax bracket. He has a net worth of about $500k. Most of his investments are currently in corporate bonds and government bonds, with nothing to offset his taxable income.

Would municipal bonds be an appropriate product for this client?

*****   Press Y for YES   Press N for NO

Press V if you'd like to VIEW previous screen.

(A)

Figure 7.8. Simulation activity for generalization practice of material already learned. (Courtesy of Catherine M. Taggart, Merrill Lynch Training Technologies).

by each of 4 girls, when the training example was 2 girls living in each of 4 houses.

Advanced games do not explicitly tell the student what skill to apply. Creative games designed for educational purposes are much like video arcade games—the goal is specified, but playing instructions are vague, and the way to reach the goal is left up to the player. The player, then, selects and applies a variety of skills from his or her repertoire in order to win the game creatively or attain a high score. Reinforcing and punishing consequences result "naturally" from the game; whatever the student does that results in more points is reinforced (by points or winning), and whatever does not lead to a successful result is punished (by few points, loss of points, or losing the game).

In a *simulation* aimed at teaching generalization, the student is given a situation and a problem and asked to solve the problem. Simulations are either static or dynamic. In a static simulation, a

CLIENT BACKGROUND

Paul Smith is a 48 year old Certified Public Accountant with a private practice. He earns about $65k, which places him in the highest tax bracket. He has a net worth of about $500k. Most of his investments are currently in corporate bonds and government bonds, with nothing to offset his taxable income.

Correct. Municipal bonds would be a good investment for this client, as he is in a high tax bracket. This usually translates to a higher taxable equivalent yield as compared with corporates or governments.

YOU EARN $150 BONUS POINTS!   YOU EARN $150 BONUS POINTS!

Press the SPACE BAR to present product to client.

(B)

Figure 7.8. Continued. (Figure 7.8C continued on p. 178.)

student's response does not alter the course of the simulation, but the student's response alters a dynamic simulation.

A *static simulation* may be presented on one or multiple frames. One frame may present an entire problem and the student asked to solve the problem. The next frame presents another entire problem with query. A static simulation may also be *event-stepped*, which means that part of the situation is presented on one frame, a student is queried about that part, then the next event occurs on the subsequent frame. Several frames may be used before the entire situation is presented; in fact, some simulations last for hours. Queries to the student concern the student's understanding of the situation (such as "Why did that event happen?" and "What do you think will happen next?"), but the student does not alter the course of the simulation.

The frame in Figure 7.9 follows the frame sequence presented in Figure 4.13. The frame in Figure 7.9 represents a new event unfolding that complicates the picture of the young couple presented

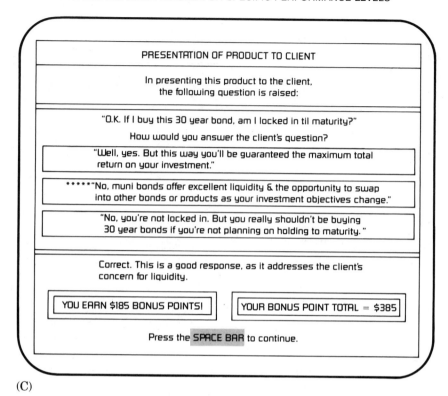

(C)

Figure 7.8. Continued.

earlier. Such complicating incidents are common indeed in the lives of the customers of stockbrokers.

In a *dynamic simulation,* the student's actions are incorporated into the problem situation. For example, the student could direct a person in a dynamic simulation to turn right (in response to a question such as "What action would you like to occur next?"). Dynamic simulations are more complex to design and program than are static simulations.

Simulations that award points for correct answers or actions and involve fantasy (as with space creatures or dragons, for example) situations resemble instructional games. However, many simulations are not instructional games. These simulations pretest the student, provide feedback during the simulation, posttest the student, generate a student record, and do not award points or involve fantasy situations.

Techniques for Proficiency Maintenance

Proficiency maintenance of skill mastery may be accomplished in three ways. First, the skill may be used in daily life, and no special CBI review or mastery maintenance program is needed. Second, the skill may become a building block for other skills. Thus it would no longer be necessary to practice the skill in isolation. The skill would be maintained at mastery levels as a component of a frequently performed more complex or generalized skill. CBI programs that build on previously learned skills thus demonstrate some amount of instructional efficiency. Third, the skill may not be used very frequently, and as time goes by, the student will forget it. A CBI proficiency maintenance program could be designed to review and practice the skill periodically. During proficiency maintenance, then, the courseware, or at least the frequency of its use, changes. Occasional review of the mastered skill ensures that the performance is at full strength when needed.

Review is important within and across lessons. CBI has been criticized by some because students seem to master, or at least complete, lessons quickly, but also seem to lose proficiency just as quickly. This situation is not the fault of CBI in general but is a problem for designers to correct.

A commonly used technique for proficiency maintenance is *review drill*. (Refer to the review drill format presented in Figure 1.2.) This type of drill is similar to the drills, games, and races used to build fluency, but different in some very important ways. All drills provide repeated practice. However, the purpose of maintenance drills is to review, whereas the purpose of fluency drills is to improve a fledgling skill. A review drill should use many of the examples and nonexamples the student was exposed to in acquisition, fluency, and generalization exercises. It is important that a review drill include exercises of varying levels of difficulty.

In review drills, consequent events need not be delivered after every response. The student enters a review drill having already attained mastery at some point in the past. Continuous feedback is unnecessary. In addition to the less frequent delivery of feedback, another important aspect of proficiency maintenance drills is a change in the nature of the consequences. The consequences should be as natural as possible, that is, related to the natural consequences in performing the skill. If the student makes frequent errors in maintenance drills, it becomes obvious that maintenance drills have been presented too early, and that acquisition, fluency-

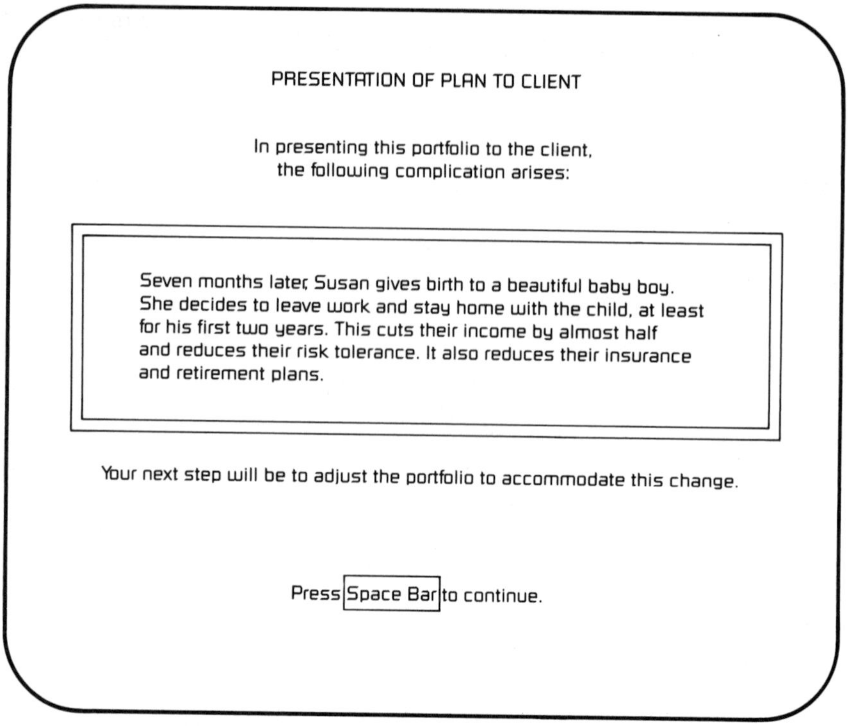

PRESENTATION OF PLAN TO CLIENT

In presenting this portfolio to the client,
the following complication arises:

Seven months later, Susan gives birth to a beautiful baby boy.
She decides to leave work and stay home with the child, at least
for his first two years. This cuts their income by almost half
and reduces their risk tolerance. It also reduces their insurance
and retirement plans.

Your next step will be to adjust the portfolio to accommodate this change.

Press Space Bar to continue.

Figure 7.9. New event introduced into a static simulation used for generalization practice. (Courtesy of Catherine M. Taggart, Merrill Lynch Training Technologies.)

building, or generalization exercises should be introduced. If proficiency is easy to maintain, however, one may assume that acquisition and fluency building have been well designed. During this time of maintenance, then, new concepts and skills may be introduced in other acquisition programs.

Study Questions

Definition Questions

1. Describe an acquisition-level performance.
2. What are characteristics of antecedent and consequent events in acquisition-level frames?
3. Describe performance in the fluency-building stage.

4. What are characteristics of antecedent and consequent events in fluency-building frames?
5. Describe a generalization performance.
6. Describe the three types of generalization.
7. What are characteristics of antecedent and consequent events used to foster the three types of generalization?
8. Describe a performance in proficiency maintenance.
9. What are characteristics of antecedent and consequent events in proficiency maintenance?

Discussion Questions

1. Design a short frame series that illustrates teaching examples and nonexamples of a concept. Be able to support your design.
2. What are ways in which drill can be made interesting?
3. When in a lesson should generalization practice begin? Why?
4. What are similarities and differences among drill for fluency building, generalization, and proficiency maintenance?
5. Design a courseware sequence used to teach a concept of your choice for each performance level.

CHAPTER 8

Evaluating and Revising CBI

The main topics in this chapter are:

• *Structural evaluation of CBI using a checklist*
• *Functional evaluation of CBI using student performance measures*
• *Determining cost-effectiveness*
• *User opinion in CBI evaluation*
• *Revising CBI*

Introduction

A thorough courseware evaluation includes four components: (1) evaluation of the structure of the lesson, (2) the functional or training effectiveness of the lesson, (3) user opinions, and (4) the dollar costs weighed against the training effectiveness of the lesson. These four evaluation components are described in this chapter. In addition, techniques for revising courseware based on the results of evaluations are described.

A *structural evaluation* is an assessment of the structure and appearance of the lesson. A structural evaluation is useful in predicting how well the courseware will teach without actually having students test it. In addition, if the courseware is not teaching effectively, a structural evaluation identifies weaknesses that might account for lack of effectiveness.

A *functional evaluation* tests how well the courseware teaches. In a functional evaluation, a student's skill level is measured before and after completing the course to determine how effective was the courseware. A functional evaluation is the most important evaluation component, although a functional evaluation alone is inadequate.

Student and teacher *opinion* about the courseware should be assessed. If users do not like the courseware or find it boring for some reason, the courseware will not be used, no matter how effective it may be according to the numbers.

Finally, *cost-effectiveness* is an important measure in evaluating CBI. Considering the dollar costs allows one to decide if a courseware module is worth the money. Weighing costs against training effectiveness leads to wise decision making.

Courseware evaluation should be conducted at least twice. The first evaluation is conducted to guide courseware revisions before the courseware is released. These are *formative evaluations*, conducted during product formation. A designer conducts structural evaluations and tests the courseware on associates or a small number of test students to see if the courseware's teaching or functional effects are acceptable. User opinions are also gathered at this time. The designer then works to correct the courseware's deficiencies before releasing the product.

The second evaluation, called a *summative evaluation*, is conducted with potential courseware purchasers, potential users, and courseware researchers on a product that is final. The data from summative evaluations guide purchase and use decisions. The summative evaluation determines if the product is acceptable or if the product is better than another product or instructional method.

Table 8.1 summarizes the types of evaluation most suited for formative and summative evaluations. This chapter presents sample formats for all these courseware evaluations. The reader should adapt these formats by lengthening or shortening them to suit each particular application.

Structural Evaluation Using Checklists

A structural evaluation is conducted using a checklist of items that are important in the courseware. The evaluator looks for the adequacy of each item in the courseware under study and notes how the courseware scores. Formative structural evaluations help the designer evaluate the courseware and identify elements that need revision. Summative structural evaluations help make the courseware purchase decision.

A structural evaluation does not evaluate student performance but is important in several circumstances. First, checklist items provide some method of assessing courseware aspects not touched by evaluations of student performance. Knowing that students do well using the courseware does not address the quality of the displays and clarity of stated instructional objectives. A functional evaluation does not isolate specific courseware aspects which should be changed or retained, but a structural evaluation can accomplish this. Use of a comprehensive checklist therefore enriches the total courseware evaluation.

Second, functional evaluation requires skill, time, money, and access to test students. Limited resources may make functional evaluation difficult or impossible. A checklist evaluation that uncovers strengths and weaknesses may be used to predict generally how students will perform using the courseware.

Finally, potential purchasers with only limited access to the product may wish to evaluate the courseware quickly. In all these circumstances, a structural courseware evaluation assumes an important role.

Structural Evaluation Procedures

The evaluator considers each item on the structural evaluation checklist and determines if the courseware is acceptable or unacceptable on each item. Each evaluator must determine the definitions of acceptable and unacceptable, depending on the intended use of the courseware. Instead of assessing all the items on one run-through of the courseware, an evaluator should critique the instructional program by running it more than once, each time focusing on certain items. At the end, the evaluator summarizes the data and makes a decision. A designer makes decisions about what aspects of the courseware to revise. A potential user decides whether or not to purchase or use the product.

TABLE 8.1 Types of Courseware Evaluation

	Time of Evaluation	
Types of Evaluation	Formative (on self or small number of students; on draft product)	Summative (on larger student sample; on final product)
Structural (Tables 8.1 through 8.15)	×	
Functional (Table 8.16)	×	×
User Opinion (Tables 8.17 and 8.18)	×	×
Cost-Effectiveness (Table 8.19)		×

Note. Table 8.20 provides a format for summarizing all four evaluations.

Categories of Structural Evaluation Items

There are four categories of structural evaluation items: (1) items of general identifying data, evidence of functional effectiveness, and courseware objectives (Tables 8.2 to 8.4); (2) items concerning qual-

TABLE 8.2 Structural Courseware Evaluation: General Identifying Information

COURSEWARE IDENTIFICATION

Evaluator: Fill in the information on the blanks below. At the end of the section is a blank for you to record whether the courseware is acceptable or not acceptable to you, based on this section of items.

_____ Title

_____ Publisher

_____ Cost for first copy

_____ Cost for additional copies

_____ Estimated cost per student

_____ Hardware required

_____ General topic, content

_____ Designate type of program: linear, branching, complex, intelligent, drill and practice, instructional game, expert system, simulation

_____ Number of lessons

_____ Number of interactions

_____ Number of tests

_____ Pretest available

_____ Posttest available

_____ Sequence of units determined by learner or computer.

_____ Sequence of content points within units determined by learner or computer

_____ Computer feedback to the student based on: response accuracy, response speed, both accuracy and speed, learning pattern, comparison of student's response to a data base

_____ Student–program interaction: menus, HELP command available, natural language query available only at menu points, mouse, joystick, other

_____ SUMMARY: ACCEPTABLE OR UNACCEPTABLE

Comments

ity of displays (Tables 8.5 to 8.7); (3) items concerning general sequencing, specific frames, and use of learning principles (Tables 8.8 to 8.10); and (4) items concerning the interactions for each student performance level (Tables 8.11 to 8.14). All the data can be summarized for purposes of making a decision, using Table 8.15.

The evaluator completes the items on courseware identification and instructional objectives by referring to the written material accompanying the courseware, or may gather the data on an initial run-through. Tables 8.2 to 8.4 present these items.

Structural evaluation checklist items for display quality are presented in Tables 8.5 to 8.7. The formative evaluator applies the items to individual displays and uses the data to change any and all displays needed. The summative evaluator makes a judgment on display quality of the entire lesson.

TABLE 8.3 Structural Courseware Evaluation: Evidence of Functional Effectiveness

EVIDENCE OF FUNCTIONAL EFFECTIVENESS

Evaluator: For each item, determine if the courseware is acceptable, unacceptable, or not applicable for your purposes. Place a mark in the correct column by each item. At the end of the section is a space for you to record if the courseware is acceptable or unacceptable to you, based on this section of items.

NA	Acc	Un-acc	
___	___	___	Training effectiveness data available
___	___	___	Program collects student performance data
___	___	___	Program stores student performance data
			Data Collected:
___	___	___	Number correct
___	___	___	Number incorrect
___	___	___	Time taken
___	___	___	Frequency correct per minute
___	___	___	Frequency incorrect per minute
___	___	___	Percent correct
___	___	___	Other performance measures
___	___	___	Remedial branches
___	___	___	Available for first, second, and third errors
___	___	___	Branch design strategy

_____ SUMMARY: ACCEPTABLE OR UNACCEPTABLE

Comments

TABLE 8.4 Structural Courseware Evaluation: Courseware Objectives

COURSEWARE OBJECTIVES

Evaluator: For each item, determine if the courseware is acceptable, unacceptable, or not applicable for your purposes. Place a mark in the correct column by each item. At the end of the section is a space for you to record if the courseware is acceptable or unacceptable to you, based on this section of items.

NA   Acc   Un-
acc

Objectives clearly stated:

____ ____ ____ In the program

____ ____ ____ In documentation

____ ____ ____ Not provided, derived by instructor

____ ____ ____ Instructional objectives (list for each):

Following lesson(s) on . . .

Given . . .

Student will . . .

Performance criteria . . .

Skill tested . . .

Performance level . . .

Motivational aspects of the courseware:

____ ____ ____ Praise available for trying as well as for correctness

____ ____ ____ Praise not overdone

____ ____ ____ Praise not too infrequent

____ ____ ____ Punishing messages are mild

____ ____ ____ Artistic enhancements

____ ____ ____ Interesting graphics

____ ____ ____ Ease of operation

____ ____ ____ Student status (e.g., cumulative correct score, time to completion) displayed

_____ SUMMARY: ACCEPTABLE OR UNACCEPTABLE

Comments

_____

_____

Tables 8.8 to 8.10 contain structural evaluation checklist items related to the general sequencing of the lesson and to the general learning principles incorporated into the courseware. The formative evaluator evaluates on a more detailed level than does the summative evaluator. The formative evaluator needs the detailed information in order to make sufficient revisions.

Tables 8.11 to 8.14 contain structural evaluation checklist items related to the structure of courseware sequences for each performance

TABLE 8.5 Structural Evaluation: Text Display

DISPLAY OF TEXT

Evaluator: For each item, determine if the courseware is acceptable, unacceptable, or not applicable for your purposes. Place a mark in the correct column by each item. At the end of the section is a space for you to record if the courseware is acceptable or unacceptable to you, based on this section of items.

NA   Acc   Un-
acc

			Format consistency (layout, color codes, audio, other) present across frame types:
___	___	___	Text presentation frames
___	___	___	Prompts, extra help
___	___	___	Response requirement signal
___	___	___	Feedback frames
___	___	___	Introduction frames
___	___	___	Review frames
___	___	___	Test frames
___	___	___	Other type _____
___	___	___	Feedback located near the answer
___	___	___	Uncluttered frames
___	___	___	Wide margins top and bottom
___	___	___	Wide margins left and right
___	___	___	Double spacing or single spacing of short paragraphs
___	___	___	Paragraphs clearly indicated
___	___	___	Important items highlighted
___	___	___	Clear color coding
			Reading ease:
___	___	___	Appropriate reading grade level
___	___	___	Clear wording
___	___	___	Upper- and lowercase letters
___	___	___	Extra space provided if all letters are in one case
___	___	___	No right justification
___	___	___	No end-of-line word hyphenation
___	___	___	Frames self-contained

_____ SUMMARY: ACCEPTABLE OR UNACCEPTABLE

Comments

_____

_____

TABLE 8.6 Structural Evaluation: Graphics Display

DISPLAY OF GRAPHICS

Evaluator: For each item, determine if the courseware is acceptable, unacceptable, or not applicable for your purposes. Place a mark in the correct column by each item. At the end of the section is a space for you to record if the courseware is acceptable or unacceptable to you, based on this section of items.

NA	Acc	Un-acc	
____	____	____	Attentional figures not distracting
____	____	____	Simplicity or high resolution used in more complex graphics
____	____	____	Figures clearly titled
____	____	____	Few codes used in figures
____	____	____	Figures self-contained
____	____	____	Other graphics enhancements used to advantage

_____ SUMMARY: ACCEPTABLE OR UNACCEPTABLE

Comments

_____

_____

TABLE 8.7 Structural Evaluation: Performance Record

STUDENT PERFORMANCE RECORD

Evaluator: For each item, determine if the courseware is acceptable, unacceptable, or not applicable for your purposes. Place a mark in the correct column by each item. At the end of the section is a space for you to record if the courseware is acceptable or unacceptable to you, based on this section of items.

NA	Acc	Un-acc	
____	____	____	Student identified by name and/or number
____	____	____	Duration (time score) given for each test or practice session
____	____	____	Error score given for each test or practice session
____	____	____	Test or practice session clearly identified
____	____	____	Summary statistics available
____	____	____	Other statistics (e.g., frequency correct per minute, percent correct) available

_____ SUMMARY: ACCEPTABLE OR UNACCEPTABLE

Comments

_____

_____

TABLE 8.8 Structural Evaluation: Overview Sequence

OVERVIEW SEQUENCE PLAN

Evaluator: For each item, determine if the courseware is acceptable, unacceptable, or not applicable for your purposes. Place a mark in the correct column by each item. At the end of the section is a space for you to record if the courseware is acceptable or unacceptable to you, based on this section of items.

NA	Acc	Un-acc	
			For procedures:
___	___	___	Whole-task plan
___	___	___	Part-task plan
___	___	___	Forward chaining
___	___	___	Backward chaining
___	___	___	All steps covered adequately
___	___	___	All steps covered accurately
			For concepts:
___	___	___	Logical sequencing
___	___	___	Content important
___	___	___	Content covered in enough depth
___	___	___	Content covered accurately
			In simulations:
___	___	___	Exercises same difficulty
___	___	___	Exercises increase in difficulty
___	___	___	Control of sequence by student or program
___	___	___	Quality of computer-generated advice

_____ SUMMARY: ACCEPTABLE OR UNACCEPTABLE

Comments

_____

_____

level. Again, the formative evaluator needs more detailed information than the summative evaluator and applies the items to each sequence. The summative evaluator evaluates the lesson as a whole.

Table 8.15 presents a format for summarizing the results of the structural evaluation. The designer notes areas of weakness. The potential purchaser makes a purchase decision if no other evaluations are involved. Later in the chapter a format is presented for reporting the results of all evaluations (structural, functional, cost-effectiveness, and user opinions) to make a final decision about the courseware.

TABLE 8.9 Structural Evaluation of Specific Frames

STRUCTURE OF INTRODUCTIONS, INTERACTIONS, REVIEWS, AND TESTS
Evaluator: For each item, determine if the courseware is acceptable, unacceptable, or not applicable for your purposes. Place a mark in the correct column by each item. At the end of the section is a space for you to record if the courseware is acceptable or unacceptable to you, based on this section of items.

NA	Acc	Un-acc	
			Sequences in introductions:
___	___	___	Introductions are identifiable
___	___	___	Introductions gain attention and interest
___	___	___	Introductions create context
			Interactions:
___	___	___	Interactions well designed
___	___	___	Interactions match the instructional objectives
___	___	___	Responses meaningful
___	___	___	Remedial branches appropriate to errors
			Reviews:
___	___	___	Review included prior to tests
___	___	___	Review given after limited number of incorrect responses
			Tests:
___	___	___	Tests presented at end of lesson
___	___	___	Tests presented at end of units
___	___	___	Items for any one test can vary from student to student or from test to retest
___	___	___	Tests reliable
___	___	___	Tests face valid
___	___	___	Tests content valid (keyed to instructional objectives, items related to interactions)
___	___	___	Other test validity available
___	___	___	Items unambiguous and clearly worded
___	___	___	Variety in short-answer items used
			Item types:
___	___	___	Multiple-choice
___	___	___	Fill in the blank with more than one letter in the answer
___	___	___	Other

_____ SUMMARY: ACCEPTABLE OR UNACCEPTABLE

Comments

TABLE 8.10   Structural Evaluation: Learning Principles

LEARNING PRINCIPLES

Evaluator: For each item, determine if the courseware is acceptable, unacceptable, or not applicable for your purposes. Place a mark in the correct column by each item. At the end of the section is a space for you to record if the courseware is acceptable or unacceptable to you, based on this section of items.

NA   Acc   Un-
              acc

Basic learning paradigm:

____ ____ ____   Material is presented

____ ____ ____   Response required

____ ____ ____   Student input mechanism

____ ____ ____   Consequence contingent on response accuracy

Reinforcement:

____ ____ ____   Praise messages

____ ____ ____   Pleasant tones

____ ____ ____   Other

Punishment:

____ ____ ____   Messages

____ ____ ____   Unpleasant Tones

____ ____ ____   Pause

____ ____ ____   Other

Shaping:

____ ____ ____   Gradual increase in difficulty:

____ ____ ____   within lesson

____ ____ ____   across lessons

____ ____ ____   Criterion for reinforcement changes as performance improves

Chaining:

____ ____ ____   Increase in number of steps performed before reinforcement
                   is delivered

Prompting:

____ ____ ____   Extra help provided before student answers

Fading:

____ ____ ____   Gradual decrease in prompts

Generalization:

____ ____ ____   Same material presented in different ways

____ ____ ____   Principles are taught

____ ____ ____   Related skills are taught

_____ SUMMARY: ACCEPTABLE OR UNACCEPTABLE

Comments

TABLE 8.11 Structural Evaluation of Acquisition Interactions

INTERACTIONS FOR ACQUISITION

Evaluator: For each item, determine if the courseware is acceptable, unacceptable, or not applicable for your purposes. Place a mark in the correct column by each item. At the end of the section is a space for you to record if the courseware is acceptable or unacceptable to you, based on this section of items.

NA	Acc	Un-acc	
			Acquisition-level sequences:
____	____	____	New content points introduced in isolation
____	____	____	Content points clearly stated
____	____	____	Frequent practice required
____	____	____	Practice items clearly cover the new point
____	____	____	Feedback is immediate
____	____	____	Feedback is mild
____	____	____	Occasional exaggerated feedback
____	____	____	Drill without feedback not introduced too early
____	____	____	Errors bring correct answer
____	____	____	Practice items first scored incorrect are represented

_____ SUMMARY: ACCEPTABLE OR UNACCEPTABLE

Comments

Functional Evaluation of CBI Using Student Performance Data

There are a number of ways to test courseware using student performance data; this section describes four. Some ways provide more convincing evidence about courseware effectiveness than others. We never prove once and for all that one form of a CBI lesson is better than another, but it is possible for us to gather pertinent evidence. This section describes how to design functional courseware evaluations. In the section we also describe strengths and weaknesses associated with each data collection procedure.

The first step in designing a functional evaluation is to specify an evaluation question. The question guides the selection of the evaluation plan. Four evaluation questions are listed below. Each

TABLE 8.12   Structural Evaluation of Fluency Building Interactions

INTERACTIONS FOR FLUENCY BUILDING

Evaluator: For each item, determine if the courseware is acceptable, unacceptable, or not applicable for your purposes. Place a mark in the correct column by each item. At the end of the section is a space for you to record if the courseware is acceptable or unacceptable to you, based on this section of items.

NA	Acc	Un-acc	
			Fluency building sequences:
____	____	____	Drill (numerous practice items administered in sequence) with feedback is used
____	____	____	Drill relates to acquisition items
____	____	____	Drill is interesting (items cleverly worded, or game format is used)
____	____	____	Response requirement increases (e.g., more responses are required for reinforcement) as fluency builds
____	____	____	Drill does not require difficult applications
____	____	____	Feedback changes words to natural consequences

_____ SUMMARY: ACCEPTABLE OR UNACCEPTABLE

Comments

_____

_____

question is associated with a particular evaluation plan. The plans are discussed in this chapter.

- Are most students successful with the courseware? Do they graduate within a specified time limit? Do they act quickly and accurately enough?
- Do most students learn more quickly and more accurately with this courseware than with some other method of instruction?
- Is this courseware useful for a particular student? Does the courseware cause the student to learn quickly and accurately?
- Is this courseware more useful than some other method for a particular student?

Functional Evaluation Procedures

A functional evaluation determines how well the courseware produces the desired student behavior change. A functional evaluation describes student performance and forms part of the rationale for

TABLE 8.13 **Structural Evaluation of Generalization Interactions**

INTERACTIONS FOR GENERALIZATION

Evaluator: For each item, determine if the courseware is acceptable, unacceptable, or not applicable for your purposes. Place a mark in the correct column by each item. At the end of the section is a space for you to record if the courseware is acceptable or unacceptable to you, based on this section of items.

NA	Acc	Un-acc	
			Generalization sequences:
____	____	____	Information on how to generalize is presented
____	____	____	Interactions foster generalization
____	____	____	Mixed practice drill (items cover the topic from a variety of perspectives) is used
____	____	____	Students may work for some time on a problem before it is solved (i.e., natural consequence received or program provides feedback)
____	____	____	Advanced games are used
____	____	____	Simulation is used

_____ SUMMARY: ACCEPTABLE OR UNACCEPTABLE

Comments

making decisions about the acceptability of the courseware. Data from formative functional evaluations performed by CBI developers are used to guide courseware revisions that improve the courseware teaching function. Data from summative functional evaluations performed by CBI user's guide courseware purchase and continued-use decisions.

A functional evaluation analyzes either one or both:

• Summary records for an entire class.
• The record of an individual student.

First, summary records for an entire class are analyzed to determine if most students passed within a time limit. If the data suggest that the average student is successful with the courseware, the courseware is acceptable. A formative evaluator using this method is satisfied if the courseware is found to be acceptable for the average student. This method is used more frequently than testing with individual students. A second use for group performance summaries involves comparing the summary records of one

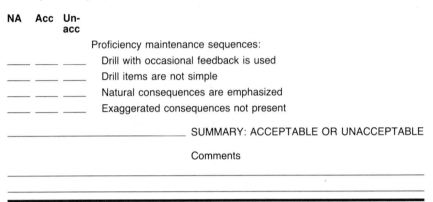

TABLE 8.14   Structural Evaluation of Proficiency Maintenance Interactions

INTERACTIONS FOR PROFICIENCY MAINTENANCE

Evaluator: For each item, determine if the courseware is acceptable, unacceptable, or not applicable for your purposes. Place a mark in the correct column by each item. At the end of the section is a space for you to record if the courseware is acceptable or unacceptable to you, based on this section of items.

NA	Acc	Un-acc	
			Proficiency maintenance sequences:
____	____	____	Drill with occasional feedback is used
____	____	____	Drill items are not simple
____	____	____	Natural consequences are emphasized
____	____	____	Exaggerated consequences not present

_____ SUMMARY: ACCEPTABLE OR UNACCEPTABLE

Comments

_____

_____

class using a particular piece of courseware to summary records of classes that used other courseware or other media. In this case, the courseware or method producing the better student performance is viewed as more acceptable. Courseware is put to a harder test when it must outperform another course or method, as opposed to demonstrating that it is effective compared to nothing.

The record of an individual student is analyzed to determine if the courseware is effective for that particular student. This involves comparing the student's record using the courseware with his or her record using another method. A summative evaluator testing courseware with an individual student is focusing very sharply on the individual student and his or her special learning needs, determining if that student can make effective use of that courseware. Taking the time to conduct an individual courseware effectiveness analysis indicates that the student is receiving special attention. A formative evaluator testing with individual students is also conducting a fine-grained analysis. A formative evaluator conducts an evaluation using individual students by watching each student perform and making notes about student performance difficulties, in order to design revisions. Such careful testing is conducted before the courseware is tested on entire classes or large groups.

TABLE 8.15 Summarizing Results of Structural Evaluation

STRUCTURAL EVALUATION SUMMARY

Evaluator: Record below the results of the four categories of structural evaluation. Summarize your overall evaluation.

NA	Acc	Un-acc	
			Category 1: General Identifying Information
___	___	___	Courseware identification (Table 8.2)
___	___	___	Evidence of functional effectiveness (Table 8.3)
___	___	___	Courseware objectives (Table 8.4)
___	___	___	Summary for category
			Category 2: Displays
___	___	___	Text (Table 8.5)
___	___	___	Graphics (Table 8.6)
___	___	___	Student performance record (Table 8.7)
___	___	___	Summary for category
			Category 3: General Sequencing/Learning Principles
___	___	___	Overview sequence plans (Table 8.8)
___	___	___	Sequences in introduction, interactions, reviews, and tests (Table 8.9)
___	___	___	Learning principles (Table 8.10)
___	___	___	Summary for category
			Category 4: Sequences for Each Performance Level
___	___	___	Acquisition sequences (Table 8.11)
___	___	___	Fluency buildling sequences (Table 8.12)
___	___	___	Generalization sequences (Table 8.13)
___	___	___	Proficiency maintenance sequences (Table 8.14)
___	___	___	Summary for category
___	___	___	Summary of Total Structural Evaluation

_____ SUMMARY: ACCEPTABLE OR UNACCEPTABLE

Comments

Four Functional Evaluation Plans

If you test courseware on a small number of individual students, you use the data to predict what effects the courseware will have with other individual students. It is hard to predict average class performance from the performance record of one student. If you test courseware on entire classes of students, you use the data to predict what effects the courseware will have with other entire classes. It is hard to predict how a particular student will perform using average class performance data. (How many constitutes a small number or a group depends on the typical group size in each specific application. A small number often means 5 or less, and a group is often at least 20.)

Thus the four functional evaluation plans are:

1. Use of one group of students to determine if the courseware is effective for groups.
2. Use of more than one group to determine if the courseware is more effective than another method, for groups.
3. Use of one student to determine if the courseware is effective for that particular student.
4. Use of one student to determine if the courseware is more effective than other methods, for that student.

Measures of Student Performance

A functional evaluation uses measures of student performance that reveal student progress and hence courseware training effectiveness. Good computer systems easily calculate these measures following a session using raw student-performance-data that were collected during the session. Otherwise, evaluators collect and summarize the data for themselves. In any case, evaluators themselves interpret the data and make decisions. Even if an expert system were available to make the decisions, a human being would check the decision and decide to accept or not accept the system's advice.

Four performance measures are useful in evaluating CBI training effectiveness: (1) percent of students completing the lesson within a time limit, (2) percent of all answers correct, (3) time spent in training, and (4) number of correct and incorrect answers per minute. Evaluations using an entire class collect data on any or all the measures. Evaluations using individual students collect data on any or all of the last three measures.

Percent of students completing the lesson is simply calculated by dividing the number of students completing the lesson by the total number of students who attempt the lesson. This measure gives an indication of dropout rates.

Percent correct answers is calculated by dividing the number of correct answers by the total number of test items (e.g., 15 correct on a 20-item test is 75 percent correct). Percent correct answers is calculated on a final exam, not on practice interactions attempted during the lesson. Percent correct answers is independent of the time spent completing the test items. It refers to accuracy only. Percent correct answers does not describe a performance as thoroughly as a measure that is based on both accuracy and time.

Time spent in instruction includes all time spent, including practice interactions and tests. Including this measure along with percent graduates and percent correct score on final exam adds depth to the functional assessment.

Frequency per minute of correct and incorrect answers are two measures that describe both the accuracy and speed of performance. If a student completed a 20-item test in 15 minutes, scored 15 correct and made 5 errors, the frequency correct is 15 correct/15 minutes, or 1 correct answer per minute. The frequency incorrect is 5 errors/15 minutes, or 0.33 incorrect per minute.

Frequency per minute correct and incorrect answers are helpful measures both when only one attempt is allowed and if repeated attempts are allowed. In the example above, 20 items were given and only the first answer per item was scored. On a 20-item with repeats allowed, a student might score 20 correct per minute, but also score 20 incorrect per minute. In cases where repeated attempts are allowed, the scores for both frequency correct and incorrect should be considered when assessing the student's progress. Good CBI generates accelerating frequencies for correct answers and decelerating frequencies for errors.

Another measure, related to frequency correct and incorrect, is useful if evaluating courseware using an individual student. *Celeration* is the change in frequency (correct or incorrect answers per minute) over time, usually calculated over a week (Pennypacker, Koenig, and Lindsley, 1972). The formula for celeration is: larger frequency/smaller frequency, then add a " × " or " / " sign to the quotient. If the frequency scored a week later is greater than the frequency of the earlier week, the ratio reflects acceleration. We symbolize acceleration with a " × " (times) sign in front of the ratio. Deceleration, when the second frequency is slower than the first frequency, is symbolized with a " / " (divide by) sign before the quotient.

The following illustrates celeration calculations. If a student scored 1 correct answer per minute on Monday and scored 5 correct answers per minute on the following Monday, performance has accelerated. The celeration in this case is 5 correct in 1 minute in week 2 divided by 1 correct in 1 minute in week 1, or × 5. A " × " sign is used because improvement was shown over time. However, if a student scored 12 correct answers per minute on Monday and scored 9 correct answers per minute a week later, a slowing or deceleration has occurred. In this case, the celeration is 12/9 with a "/" sign with the answer, or /1.3. A ⅓ drop in performance was shown.

How do you compute celeration of errors if a student scores 2 errors per minute one week and 0 errors per minute the following week? The calculation would be 2/0, but 0 cannot be used as a divisor. We find an acceptable substitute number for the 0 that lies somewhere between but not including 0 and 1. A solution is to divide 1 (a standard number in this case) by the number of minutes in the test. If 0 errors were scored in a 10-minute test, the calculation would be ⅒, or 0.1 error, so you could use 0.1 error instead of 0 errors in the fraction. If the test lasted 60 minutes, 0 errors could be scored as ¹⁄₆₀, or 0.02 error. The celeration calculation for 2 errors per minute one week on a 60-minute test and 0 errors per minute the next then becomes 2/0.02, or a /100 deceleration. The /100 celeration indicates that in this case errors decreased 100-fold. [Pennypacker, Koenig, and Lindsley (1972) suggest a similar calculation. Interested readers may refer to that handbook for information on other measures related to frequency correct and incorrect.]

Using Data from an Entire Class

As mentioned earlier, data from an entire class may be used to determine if the courseware teaches. This is done by administering a pretest to the group, implementing instruction, and administering a posttest after instruction. Students are scored on one or more performance measures: percent of students passing the test, percent correct on the test, and frequency of correct and incorrect answers per minute. Total time spent in instruction is collected and used to determine if the courseware teaches quickly enough for the situation.

The class average scores on the pretests and posttests are compared to determine if the change in scores before and after instruction is significant. Significant is defined either as "practical" or "statistical." Statistical significance is determined using inferential statistics. Statistical significance tells if the change in scores exceeds what mathematicians would attribute to chance. A statistically significant score change (in the positive direction) allows one to attribute the improved performance to use of the courseware. (Of course, it is not really all that simple. In order to believe the statistics and significance calculations, one must be satisfied with an explanation of how the scores were gathered. Conditions of pretest and posttest must be the same.)

Practical significance is more informal but no less important. In an evaluation of practical significance, the evaluator simply determines if the size of the improvement (if there is any) is adequate, defining adequate in the context of the application. A common informal criterion for "adequate" is 80 percent of students scoring 80 percent correct within the time limit. This type of evaluation tells whether the class as a whole benefited from use of the instruction. The instructor evaluating practical significance is asking "Is this courseware good enough to satisfy me? Will it help this class?"

Two or more groups of students are used to determine if courseware is more effective than some other method. For example, one group of students receives training method A and another group of similar students receives training method B. The students each complete a pretest, training, then a posttest. The group mean scores on the pretest and posttest are statistically compared. If in a hypothetical case, training group A changed from a mean of 50 percent correct to 60 percent correct, and training group B changed from 50 percent correct to 80 percent correct, if each group contained 30 students, the improvements for training group B would be significantly better than for method A. Again, the significance of the change may be determined using practical and statistical approaches.

The information provided in this chapter about evaluation using groups of students will familiarize readers and whet the appetites of some readers for more information. Readers interested in more information about groups comparison experimental designs might consult the classic Campbell and Stanley (1963) reference and Kerlinger (1973) for starters.

Using Individual Students

As mentioned earlier, courseware is tested on one student to determine if the courseware is effective for that student. One simple evaluation procedure compares the performance of one student before, during, and after instruction. First, the student is tested before instruction and may be tested repeatedly until the evaluator is convinced that the student will not progress further without instruction. Then CBI is introduced and performance is measured during instruction, which may last over several sessions, and a learning curve is generated. It is also good practice to make a follow-up measure after instruction is completed to assess retention effects of the courseware. This procedure is called an "A-B" procedure. A-B means that one procedure (A), in this case the procedure "no teaching," is used first, then the second procedure (B) is used.

However, any decisions based on an A-B evaluation are tentative, because an A-B evaluation is weak compared to other evaluation procedures. An A-B evaluation is weak because influences other than the teaching method may be responsible for any effects observed. For example, one student may require 6 days of practice with *any* method before improvements are seen, but method B is in effect only 4 days. In another case, one student may be able to learn merely through 3 days practice with the pretest, but the pretest was given on only 1 day. Then, 2 days into method B, performance improves. It would be erroneous to say that method B is responsible for the improvement.

A way to improve on the A-B evaluation is to repeat it, either with the same student in a new topic or lesson, or with more students. Repeating the A-B evaluation allows you to see if the A-B sequence produces the same effects with one student in several different topics or classrooms, perhaps at different times of the day, or with several different students. If the performance under both A or B conditions is similar each time, you increase your confidence that those are the true effects of the A or B procedures. If all A conditions (no teaching, for example) produce poor performance, but all B conditions (a CBI lesson, for example) produce good performance, you have good evidence that for that student or group of students, the B procedure produces better performance.

Several teaching methods, as opposed to one or two, may also be assessed using expanded A-B evaluations. For example, three methods [no teaching (A), teaching procedure B, and teaching procedure C] might be evaluated using an A-B-A-C design. In the first case, the sequence of teaching methods would be: no teaching, procedure B, no teaching, then procedure C. Providing that the material was of the same difficulty throughout, the instructor could determine if improvements over no teaching resulted at all, and if so, were greater using method B or C. Again, you will become more confident in the findings as they are repeated, with the same or other students, in the same or different courses.

One problem encountered in evaluating different teaching methods using the same student is that once a student has learned lesson 1, you cannot make the student forget what he or she learned, and re-teach lesson 1 with another method. It may not be fair to compare method A on lesson 1 to method B on lesson 2, because the lesson material may be very different. As before, one way around the problem is to repeat the A-B and A-C evaluations with the same student using different topics, and see if A, B, and C effects are similar each time. Another way is to repeat the A-B and A-C sequences with more students. Finally, one should keep the topics as similar as possible in the early stages of testing. However, once you have confidence in the effects of a procedure, you can begin to test it out using diverse topics. You may find that method A is better than method B no matter what the topic.

Table 8.16 presents a format for summarizing data on courseware functional effectiveness. A comprehensive text on experimental evaluation using individual subjects is Johnston and Pennypacker (1980). Interested readers may consult that book for more details.

User Opinion

In addition to structural and functional CBI evaluations, user opinion is a valuable source of evaluation data. Evaluators collect user opinions by interviewing students and teachers for their opinions about the courseware. User opinion highlights strong and weak points of the program and addresses the issues of consumer appeal and willingness to accept the courseware. Tables 8.17 and 8.18 present instructor and student courseware opinion interview formats. In many cases, the evaluator makes personal contact with

TABLE 8.16 Summary of Functional Evaluation Data

COURSEWARE EFFECTIVENESS

Evaluator: Summarize the findings from courseware effectiveness evaluations below. If data are unavailable, write "N/A." At the bottom of the page is a place for you to determine if the data are acceptable or not acceptable to you.

_____ Class graduate rate

_____ Class improvement in percent correct

_____ Class improvement in frequency correct

_____ Class improvement in frequency incorrect

_____ Class average time spent in instruction

_____ How courseware compared to other methods

_____ Individual student improvement in percent correct

_____ Individual student improvement in frequency correct

_____ Individual student improvement in frequency incorrect

_____ Student total time spent in training

_____ How courseware compared to other methods for that student

_____ SUMMARY: ACCEPTABLE OR UNACCEPTABLE

Comments

the users and does not rely only on the user's written comments. The evaluator makes a decision about scheduling personal contacts in addition to written comments, depending on resources available and expected gains.

Evaluating Cost-Effectiveness

Cost-effectiveness translates into the amount of training you get for the dollar. Cost-effectiveness of a CBI module involves (1) specifying the costs of developing, producing, testing, and revising the module, then (2) determining how much "one unit of training effectiveness" costs. These costs can then be compared to the costs of other instructional procedures which teach the same instructional objectives. (The term "cost/training effectiveness" used by some authors is synonymous with the term "cost-effectiveness" used in this book.)

Step 1: Determining Costs of CBI

Determining what costs to use is the first step in a cost-effectiveness evaluation. There is no one set of costs that must be assessed. Evaluators select the costs that apply in their own situation. For example, in determining the cost of off-the-shelf courseware, no development costs are considered. However, organizations that develop their own courseware must consider the cost of development time in determining how much the courseware costs.

Seidel and Wagner (1979) specified a list of cost categories for use in determining CBI costs: development, procurement and production, and operations and maintenance costs. Development costs include research, design, development, test, evaluation, and management. Procurement costs involve production, all purchasing, and installation. Operations and maintenance costs include training for site personnel and administration. For a large-scale CBI system with an operations period of 8 years, development may take up to 6 years and procurement up to 1 year. At the other end of the spectrum, short practice CBI modules may be developed in less than a month, be purchased in less than a month, and be useful in a classroom for a year, depending on frequency of use. The list of costs for the large system will obviously be much longer than for the classroom module.

A list of these costs includes:

TABLE 8.17 Instructor Opinion Interview

INSTRUCTOR OPINION INTERVIEW

Instructor: For each item, determine if the courseware is acceptable, unacceptable, or not applicable for your purposes. Place a mark in the correct column by each item. At the end of the section is a space for you to record if the courseware is acceptable or unacceptable to you, based on this section of items. There is also space for you to write suggestions for improvement. Thank you for your time.

NA	Acc	Un-acc	
___	___	___	Objectives clearly stated
___	___	___	Objectives important
___	___	___	Accompanying documentation is thorough
___	___	___	Effective in teaching
___	___	___	Well designed with respect to important learning principles
___	___	___	An efficient use of time
___	___	___	Held student interest
___	___	___	Quality of graphics
___	___	___	Clarity of frame format
___	___	___	Important material emphasized
___	___	___	Reading grade level appropriate
___	___	___	Wording clear
___	___	___	Easy to use
___	___	___	For program-controlled sequences, sequence of topics was justified
___	___	___	Context of new material was made clear
___	___	___	Generalization practice was included
___	___	___	Tests were content valid
___	___	___	Practice or testing was frequent enough
___	___	___	Tests were comprehensive

_____SUMMARY: ACCEPTABLE OR UNACCEPTABLE

Comments

1. Development.

* All equipment purchased, including the cost to maintain the equipment throughout the development phase.
* Cost to maintain the facility where development takes place.
* All costs of development, including engineering and research (includes labor and materials).
* Costs of testing.

TABLE 8.18 Student Opinion Interview

STUDENT OPINION INTERVIEW

Student: For each item, determine if the courseware is acceptable, unacceptable, or not applicable for your purposes. Place a mark in the correct column by each item. At the end of the section is a space for you to record if the courseware is acceptable or unacceptable to you, based on this section of items. There is also space for you to write in suggestions for improvement. Thank you for your time.

**NA Acc Un-
          acc**

___ ___ ___ The purpose and instructional objectives of the courseware
               were clear to me

___ ___ ___ The instruction centered around the objectives

___ ___ ___ The subject matter was important

___ ___ ___ Amount of practice on each topic/subtopic

___ ___ ___ Held my interest

___ ___ ___ Graphics were interesting or effective

___ ___ ___ Ease of use

___ ___ ___ Tests were fair

___ ___ ___ Difficulty level

___ ___ ___ Wording of feedback messages

_____SUMMARY: ACCEPTABLE OR UNACCEPTABLE

Comments:

2. Procurement and production (e.g., production, purchase, installation costs).

* Production.
* Labor/management costs involved in conducting acceptance tests, purchasing, and installing the courseware.
* Courseware purchase cost.
* Costs of training the initial group of site management personnel.

3. Operations and maintenance.

* Cost per hour for student access multiplied by number of use hours.
* Cost for integrating CBI (include cost of disposing old material).
* Cost of expertise required to run and monitor the course.
* Effects on dropout rate.

* Cost of space required.
* Cost of other resource requirements.
* Cost of equipment repair.

CBI costs vary widely. Development costs and hardware purchase account for most of the cost (Chambers & Sprecher, 1980), as opposed to procurement and operations. Development time ranges from 50 to 500 hours of developers' labor per hour of CBI contact time, and cost per student hour ranges from $0.50 to $28.50 (Chambers & Sprecher, 1980). A rule of thumb figure is 200 hours of development time for 1 hour of conventional CBI (Woolf & Cunningham, 1987). The 200 hours (5 workweeks) might be broken into 1 to 2 weeks of design, 2 to 3 weeks of programming, and 1 week of test and revision. The more novel the subject matter and the smarter the system, the greater the development time required. In addition, a courseware development team takes longer to develop the first module than it does later modules.

Intelligent CBI takes longer to produce, but probably because it is new. As flexibility and innovative hardware and software configurations (e.g., digitized terrain maps, large-screen display, videodisk) are added to intelligent CBI simulations, development times increase, into several thousands of hours. (There are no published data on this; this is based on the author's experience.) However, as more precedents become available, development times should shorten. It must also be kept in mind that an intelligent CBI simulation can provide many more than 1 hour's worth of instruction.

Step 2: Determining Cost-Effectiveness

There are many formulas for determining cost-effectiveness. The formulas all divide dollar costs by some measure of training effectiveness. In this section we describe two useful cost-effectiveness formulas. The first formula defines training effectiveness as number of graduates. The formula yields the cost per student completing the module (Seidel and Wagner, 1979). This formula distributes all costs to only those students who complete the course, so the cost per graduate increases with the dropout rate.

$$\text{Cost-effectiveness} = \frac{\text{Costs}}{\text{Total number of graduates}}$$

The other formula defines training effectiveness as number of instructional hours of use. It calculates the cost of one instructional hour and does not consider the number of graduates (Seidel &

TABLE 8.19 Evaluation of Cost-Effectiveness

COST-EFFECTIVENESS EVALUATION

Evaluator: Fill in available cost and training data, and calculate the cost- and training-effectiveness ratio. At the bottom, determine if the cost- and training-effectiveness ratio is acceptable or unacceptable to you.

$ _____ Development costs

$ _____ Production and procurement costs

$ _____ Operations and maintenance costs

$ _____ TOTAL COST

_____ Number of course graduates

_____ Number of instructional hours

_____ Other measure of training-effectiveness

_____ Divide cost by training-effectiveness measure

_____ SUMMARY: ACCEPTABLE OR UNACCEPTABLE

Comments

TABLE 8.20 Courseware Evaluation Summary

OVERALL COURSEWARE EVALUATION

Evaluator: Enter the results of courseware evaluations. Then determine if the courseware is acceptable or unacceptable, depending on your specific situation. Some evaluations may be more important to you than others; weight the four categories according to your own specific situation.

NA	Acc	Un-acc	
___	___	___	Summary of structural evaluation (Table 8-15)
___	___	___	Summary of functional evaluation (Table 8-16)
___	___	___	Summary of user opinion (Tables 8-17 and 8-18)
___	___	___	Summary of cost-effectiveness evaluation (Table 8-19)

_____ SUMMARY

Comments

Wagner, 1979). Cost per hour decreases as the courseware is used over and over.

$$\text{Cost-effectiveness} \ = \ \frac{\text{Costs}}{\text{Total number of instructional hours of use}}$$

An evaluator can generate cost-effectiveness ratios depending on what aspect of training-effectiveness is important to the evaluator. For example, if training-effectiveness is defined as percent improvement from pretest to posttest, the applicable cost/training-effectiveness ratio is: cost divided by percent improvement.

Table 8.19 presents a format for summarizing the cost-effectiveness of courseware.

Making an Overall Decision

Table 8.20 presents a format for combining the information from the four evaluation sources in order to make a decision. This format helps the evaluator decide if the courseware overall is adequate or not. The evaluator organizes available data using a format, but the decision is made by the evaluator. For example, the evaluator may decide that functional effectiveness is more important than courseware structure and will not hesitate to buy courseware that is functionally effective even if it had scored inadequate on the structural evaluation. Another evaluator may decide, however, that items on the structural evaluation such as display quality are so important that courseware inadequate in display quality would not be purchased. Another evaluator might decide not to purchase courseware that users did not like, no matter how high it scored on other evaluations.

Figure 8.1 presents a decision aid for evaluating two courseware packages, given dollar costs and training-effectiveness data. For example, if one package costs less and has the same effectiveness as another package, buy the less costly package.

Revising CBI

How CBI writers modify their courseware as a function of evaluation data is an interesting, yet unresearched area. In the absence

		EFFECTIVENESS		
		Less	Same	More
COST	Less	?	+	+
	Same	—	?	+
	More	—	—	?

+ Adopt
— Reject
? Uncertain

Figure 8.1. Decision diagram for evaluating the relative effectiveness and cost of two instructional methods (from J. Orlansky, personal communication, October 16, 1987).

of research on this topic, the suggested approach is to collect as much evaluation data as possible to present as thorough an assessment as possible to the courseware designer. The designer could then determine the types of revisions needed, in line with the discussion below.

Making Structural Changes

If the structure of the courseware has been downgraded on an evaluation, the designer should revise accordingly. Revise all frames and graphics that do not come up to standard. Correct sequences as necessary.

Revising to Improve Function

If the courseware is not teaching, the designer should offer solutions. In case this happens, the designer should consider these potential causes:

- Is the course being used in the environment for which it was designed? Do the test students represent the students who will use the courseware? Sometimes advanced students or even instructors are offered as test subjects. Use of a

pretest that screens out high scoring students is advised.
- Does the lesson "have its facts straight?" Are there content errors?
- Do the instructional objectives match the content to be taught? Do test items match the objectives?
- Are topics taught in the best sequence? Do easier topics precede more difficult ones? Do the topics build hierarchically? Is too much being attempted within a lesson?
- Is the sequencing of instructional events within topic sound? Are there enough interactions? Are there enough tests? Is there enough explanation before an interaction is required? Is there any way for a student to get help? Are the feedback messages helpful? Is the lesson adaptive?
- Are the menu structure and other dialogue devices causing problems? Are the displays easy to use? Is the student performance display causing problems by not providing enough reporting back to the student of his or her progress?
- Is the program actually running as it should? Is it "crashing?" Are software glitches angering the students so that they no longer pay attention to the lesson?
- Are accompanying documents providing needed information? Does the student know when to use the documents?
- Was the evaluation team in the way? Did its presence cause the test students to feel "watched?"

Revising to Improve Opinions

Reports of overall poor user opinion must be investigated. Are there problems with student or teacher opinions about the courseware? Are there recurring themes in their opinions? What changes do they recommend? Revise as necessary in line with their suggestions.

Students who have done well with a CBI lesson should report that they liked the CBI because their efforts have been reinforced. But this is not always the case. Successful students may still report, for example, that what they learned was irrelevant or too easy. They may complain about displays and formats. They may have disliked the feedback.

Students who have not progressed may report that the lesson was a waste of time. The lesson may have been too advanced or too easy. The displays may have been tedious or the format too repetitive. At any rate, students who disliked the course *and* who did not show progress have legitimate and important complaints. The designer must consider revising factors affecting functional effectiveness as well as user opinion.

Improving Cost-Effectiveness

Problems with cost-effectiveness can be relieved. Cost-effectiveness formulas consider dollar costs and training-effectiveness. Thus the cost-effectiveness ratio can be improved by either increasing the number of training successes or reducing the cost of operations (if development costs are already complete), or both. Training successes may increase as a function of other revisions suggested by other evaluations. The cost of operations could be decreased by improving the maintenance record of the courseware.

Study Questions

Definition Questions

1. Describe the four components of a courseware evaluation.
2. What are the differences between formative and summative courseware evaluations?
3. Describe four functional evaluation plans.
4. Describe revision tactics if problems are discovered with any of the four evaluation components.
5. If a new CBI system is a little more costly but produces much better learning than your present system, would you buy the system? Why?

Discussion Questions

1. As a teacher, are you justified in saying that any one student will be effective in a particular CBI course, based on the fact that the average student in a previous class passed that course within the time limit? Justify your answer.
2. As a school administrator, do you want to see performance records from one or two students or from classes of students when deciding whether to buy 50 copies of a new piece of courseware? Why?
3. If the class scores 21 percent correct on the pretest and 89 pecent correct on the posttest following use of a CBI package that provides instruction in a relatively simple skill, would you say that the courseware was effective? Why? What about 23 percent correct on the pretest and 60 percent on the posttest for a CBI package that provided instruction in a very difficult skill? Why?
4. If one student scored 1 correct per minute on a 5-minute pretest, and with instruction came to score 35 correct per minute on the posttest, would you say that the courseware was effective? Why? What evidence is needed?

5. Practice evaluating a courseware package using the evaluation formats provided.

6. A great deal of instructional software is sold in retail stores. How would you decide what to buy if you went in to buy something for a class you instruct? Or to buy something for your child to use at home?

7. Let's say that you have commissioned a CBI designer to develop some courseware for a new class in problem solving in graduate-level physics. How would you expect to interact with the designer in order to evaluate his or her progress? Are there things you could do to ensure that the courseware will be exactly what you were looking for?

References

Allen, J. A., Hays, R. T., & Buffardi, L. C. (1986). Maintenance training simulator fidelity and individual differences in transfer of training. *Human Factors, 28*, 497–509.

Anastasi, A. (1988). *Psychological testing* (6th ed.). New York: Macmillan.

Aronis, J. M., & Katz, S. (1984). RICHARD: An interactive computer program for rhetorical invention. *Educational Technology, 14*(11), 26–30.

Bailey, J. S., Hughes, R. G., & Jones, W. E. (1980). *Application of backward chaining to air to surface weapons delivery training* (Tech. Rep. No. 79–63). Air Force Human Resources Laboratory.

Becker, W. C., Engelmann, S., & Thomas, D. R. (1975). *Teaching 2: Cognitive learning and instruction.* Chicago: Science Research Associates.

Bijou, S., & Baer, D. (1978). *Behavior analysis of child development.* Englewood Cliffs, NJ: Prentice-Hall.

Birren, J. E., Woods, A. M., & Williams, M. V. (1980). Behavioral slowing with age: Causes, organization, and consequences. In L. W. Poon (Ed.), *Aging in the 1980s: Psychological issues.* Washington, DC: American Psychological Association.

Bork, A. (1984). Educational and computers: The situation today and some possible futures. *T.H.E. Journal, 12*(3), 92–97.

Born, D. G., & Whelan, P. (1973). Some descriptive characteristics of student performance in PSI and lecture classes. *Psychological Record, 23*, 145–152.

Bransford, J. D. (1979). *Human cognition: Learning, understanding, and remembering.* Belmont, CA: Wadsworth.

Bransford, J. D., & Johnson, M. K. (1972). Contextual prerequisites for understanding: Some investigations of comprehension and recall. *Journal of Verbal Learning and Verbal Behavior, 11*, 717–726.

Briggs, L. J., & Wager, W. W. (1981). *Handbook of procedures for the design of instruction* (2nd ed.). Englewood Cliffs, NJ: Educational Technology Publications.

Brown, J. S., Burton, R. R., & deKleer, J. (1982). Pedagogical, natural language and knowledge engineering techniques in SOPHIE I, II, and III. In D. Sleeman and J. S. Brown (Eds.), *Intelligent tutoring systems.* New York: Academic Press.

Bunderson, C. W. (1981). Courseware. In H. F. O'Neil, Jr. (Ed.), *Computer-based instruction: A state-of-the-art assessment.* New York: Academic Press.

Burton, R. R. (1982). Diagnosing bugs in a simple procedural skill. In D. Sleeman & J. S. Brown (Eds.), *Intelligent tutoring systems.* New York: Academic Press.

Burton, R. R., & Brown, J. S. (1979). Toward a natural-language capability for computer-assisted instruction. In H. O'Neil (Ed.), *Procedures for instructional system development*. New York: Academic Press.

Burton, R. R., & Brown, J. S. (1982). An investigation of computer coaching for informal learning activities. In D. Sleeman & J. S. Brown (Eds.), *Intelligent tutoring systems*. New York: Academic Press.

Campbell, D. T., & Stanley, J. C. (1963). *Experimental and quasi-experimental designs for research*. Chicago: Rand McNally.

Chambers, J. A., & Sprecher, J. W. (1980). Computer-assisted instruction: Current trends and critical issues. *Communications of the ACM, 23*, 332–342. Reprinted in D. F. Walker and R. D. Hess (Eds.), *Instructional software: Principles and perspectives for design and use*. Belmont, CA: Wadsworth, 1984.

Chapman, R. S., Dollaghan, C., Kenworthy, O. T., & Miller, J. F. (1983). Microcomputer testing and teaching of verb meaning: What's easy and what's hard? In A. C. Wilkinson (Ed.), *Classroom computers and cognitive science*. New York: Academic Press.

Chase, P. (1985). Designing courseware: Prompts from behavioral instruction. *Behavior Analyst, 8*, 65–76.

Clancy, W. J. (1983). GUIDON. *Journal of Computer-Based Instruction, 10*, 8–15.

Collins, A. M. (1974). *Comparison of two teaching strategies in computer-assisted instruction* (BBN Rep. No. 2885). Cambridge, MA: Bolt, Beranek, and Newman.

Cook, D. A. (1983, October). Questioning the information transmission model. *Data Training*.

Cook, D. A. (1984, April). An authoring system's hardest test. *Data Training*.

Criswell, E. L., Swezey, R. W., Allen, J. A., & Hays, R. T. (1984). *Human factors analysis of two prototype Army maintenance training and evaluation system (AMTESS) devices* (SAIC Report No. 84-11-178). McLean, VA: Science Applications International.

Criswell, E. L., Williford, R., & Smith, M. (1987). *Design specification for product to estimate manpower requirements of system designs* (SAIC Rep. No. 87-1776). McLean, VA: Science Applications International.

Dellalana, C. M. (1985). Student response data analysis: Planning for its incorporation into courseware design. *Computers in the Schools, 2*, 91–96.

Diffrient, N., Tilley, A. R., & Harman, D. (1981). *Human Scale*. Cambridge, MA: MIT Press.

Duchastel, P., & Waller, R. (1979, November). Pictorial illustration in instructional texts. *Educational Technology*, pp. 21–25.

Eberts, R., & Brock, J. F. (1984). Computer applications to instruction. *Human Factors Review, 1984*, 262–284.

Eberts, R., & Brock, J. F. (1987). Computer-assisted and computer-managed instruction. In G. Salvendy (Ed.), *Handbook of human factors*. New York: Wiley.

Englemann, S., & Carnine, D. (1982). *Theory of instruction: Principles and applications*. New York: Irvington.

Fleischman, E. (1984). *Taxonomy of human performance.* New York: Academic Press.

Fletcher, D. (in press). Intelligent training systems in the military. In G. W. Hoppel and S. J. Andriole (Eds.), *Defense applications of artificial intelligence: Progress and prospects.* Lexington, MA: Lexington Books.

Foehr, J., & Cross, T. (1986). *The soft side of software: A management approach to computer documentation.* New York: Wiley.

Fredericksen, N. (1984). Implications of cognitive theory for instruction in problem solving. *Review of Educational Research, 54,* 363–407.

Frye, C. (1980). *PLANIT reference handbook.* Portland, OR: Frye Software Unlimited.

Futrell, M. K., & Geisert, P. (1984). *The well-trained computer.* Englewood Cliffs, NJ: Educational Technology Publications.

Gagne, R. M. (1977). *The conditions of learning* (3rd ed.). New York: Holt, Rinehart and Winston.

Gagne, R. M., & Briggs, L. J. (1979). *Principles of instructional design* (2nd ed.). New York: Holt, Rinehart and Winston.

Galitz, W. O. (1981). *Handbook of screen format design.* Wellesley, MA: QED Information Sciences.

Gollin, E. S. (1970). An organism oriented concept of development. *Merill-Palmer Quarterly of Behavior and Development, 16,* 246–252.

Gould, J. D., Alfaro, L., Barnes, V., Finn, R., Grischkowsky, N., & Minuto, A. (1987). Reading is slower from CRT displays than from paper: Attempts to isolate a single-variable explanation. *Human Factors, 29,* 269–299.

Hall, K. A. (1983). Content structuring and question asking for computer-based education. *Journal of Computer-Based Instruction, 10,* 1–7.

Halpin, S. M., & Moses, F. L. (1987). Improving human performance through the application of intelligent systems. In S. J. Andriole (Ed.), *Artificial intelligence and national defense.* Washington, DC: AFCEA International Press.

Hays, R. T., & Singer, M. J. (in press). *Simulation fidelity in training system design.* New York: Springer-Verlag.

Heines, J. M. (1984). *Screen design strategies for computer-assisted instruction.* Bedford, MA: Digital Press.

Heines, J. M. (1985). I do windows. *Training News,* Winegarten Publications.

Helm, V. (1984). *Software quality and copyright: Issues in computer-assisted instruction.* Washington, DC: Association for Educational Communications and Technology.

Hollan, J., Hutchins, E., & Weitzman, L. (1984, Summer). Steamer: An interactive inspectable simulation-based training system. *AI Magazine.*

Holland, J. G., & Skinner, B. F. (1961). *The analysis of behavior.* New York: McGraw-Hill.

Johnson, K. R., & Chase, P. H. (1981). Behavior analysis in instructional design: A functional typology of verbal tasks. *The Behavior Analyst, 4,* 103–121.

Johnson, K. R., & Ruskin, R. S. (1977). *Behavioral instruction: An evaluative review.* Washington, DC: American Psychological Association.

Johnston, J. M., & Pennypacker, H. S. (1980). *Strategies and tactics of human behavioral research.* Hillsdale, NJ: Lawrence Erlbaum.

Kerlinger, F. N. (1973). *Foundations of behavioral research* (2nd ed.). New York: Holt, Rinehart and Winston.

Klare, G. R. (1974–75). Assessing readability. *Reading Research Quarterly, 10,* 62–102.

Klatzky, R. (1980). *Human memory: Structures and processes* (2nd ed.). San Francisco: W. H. Freeman.

Kulik, J. A., Bangert, R. L., & Williams, G. W. (1983). Effects of computer-based teaching on secondary school students. In D. F. Walker and R. D. Hess (Eds.), *Instructional software.* Belmont, CA: Wadsworth.

Lindsley, O. R. (1982, May). *Microprocessors, behavior analysis, and standard celeration charting.* Address to the Eighth Annual Convention of the Association for Behavior Analysis, Milwaukee, WI.

Macdonald, N. H., Frase, L. T., Gingrich, P. S., & Keenan, S. A. (1982). The Writer's Workbench: Computer aids for text analysis. *IEEE Transactions on Communications, COM30,* 105–110.

MacLachlan, J. (1986). Psychologically based techniques for improving learning within computerized tutorials. *Journal of Computer-Based Instruction, 13,* 65–70.

McCormick, E. J. (1976). Job and task analysis. In M. D. Dunnette (Ed.), *Handbook of industrial and organizational psychology.* Skokie, IL: Rand McNally.

Miller, G. A. (1956). The magical number seven, plus or minus two: Some limits on our capacity for processing information. *Psychological Review, 63,* 81–97.

Nash, E. L. (1982). *Direct marketing: strategy, planning, execution.* New York: McGraw-Hill.

Orwig, G. (1983). *Creating computer programs for learning.* Reston, VA: Reston.

Pask, Gordon. (1984). Review of conversation theory. *Educational Communication and Technology, 32,* 3–40.

Pennypacker, H. S. (1978). The computer as a management tool in systems of personalized instruction. *Journal of Personalized Instruction, 3,* 147–150.

Pennypacker, H. S., Koenig, C. H., & Lindsley, O. R. (1972). *Handbook of the standard behavior chart.* Kansas City, Precision Media.

Piaget, J. (1964). Development and learning. In R. Ripple and V. Rockcastle (Eds.), *Piaget rediscovered.* Ithaca, NY: Cornell University Press.

Pliske, R. H., Gade, P. A., & Johnson, R. M. (1984). *Analysis and interpretation of computer adaptive screening test (CAST) scores* (Personnel Utilization Technical Area Working Paper 84–8). Alexandria, VA: U.S. Army Research Institute for the Behavioral and Social Sciences.

Ramsey, H. R., & Atwood, M. E. (1979). *Human factors in computer systems: A review of the literature* (Science Applications Rep. No. 79-111-DEN). Englewood, CO: Science Applications.

Rehe, H. F. (1974). *Typography: How to make it more legible.* Carmel, IN: Design Research International.

Reynolds, L. (1982). Display problems for teletext. In D. H. Jonassen, (Ed.), *The technology of text: Principles for structuring, designing, and displaying text.* Englewood Cliffs, NJ: Educational Technology Publications.

Ross, S. M. (1983). Increasing the meaningfulness of quantitative material by adapting context to student background. *Journal of Educational Psychology, 75,* 519–529.

Ross, S. M. (1984). Matching the lesson to the student: Alternative adaptive designs for individualized learning systems. *Journal of Computer-Based Instruction, 11,* 42–48.

Ross, S. M., & Rakow, E. A. (1981). Learner control versus program control as adaptive strategies for selection of instructional support on math rules. *Journal of Educational Psychology, 73,* 745–753.

Sands, W. A., & Gade, P. A. (1983). An application of computer adaptive testing in U.S. Army recruiting. *Journal of Computer-Based Instruction, 10,* 87–89.

Schank, R., & Abelson, R. (1977). *Scripts, plans, goals and understanding: An inquiry into human knowledge structures.* Hillsdale, NJ: Lawrence Erlbaum.

Schloss, P. J., Schloss, C. N., & Cartwright, G. P. (1984). Efficacy of four ratios of questions and highlights to text in computer assisted instruction modules. *Journal of Computer-Based Instruction, 11,* 103–106.

Schloss, P. J., Sindelar, P. T., Cartwright, G. P., & Schloss, C.N. (1986). Efficacy of higher cognitive and factual questions in computer assisted instruction modules. *Journal of Computer-Based Instruction, 13,* 75–79.

Seidel, R. J., & Wagner, H. (1979). A cost-effectiveness specification. In H. O'Neil (Ed.), *Procedures for instructional system development.* New York: Academic Press.

Skinner, B. F. (1957). *Verbal behavior.* New York: Appleton-Century-Crofts.

Skinner, B. F. (1968). *The technology of teaching.* New York: Appleton-Century-Crofts.

Skinner, B. F. (1984). The shame of American education. *American Psychologist, 39,* 947–954.

Sleeman, D., & Brown, J. (Eds.). (1982). *Intelligent tutoring systems.* New York: Academic Press.

Spradlin, J. E., Karlan, G. R., & Wetherby, B. (1976). Behavior analysis, behavior modification, and developmental disabilities. In L.L. Lloyd (Ed.), *Communication assessment and intervention Strategies.* Baltimore: University Park Press.

Steinberg, E. R. (1984). *Teaching computers how to teach.* Hillsdale, NJ: Lawrence Erlbaum.

Stephens, K. (1985, June). *State notation and a top-down instructional design methodology.* Paper presented at the Eleventh Annual Convention of the Association for Behavior Analysis, Columbus, OH.

Streufert, S., & Swezey, R. W. (1986). *Complexity, managers, and organizations.* Orlando, FL: Academic Press.

Swezey, R. S., Streufert, S., Criswell, E. L., Unger, K. W., & van Rijn, P. (1984). *Development of a computer simulation for assessing decision-mak-*

ing style using cognitive complexity theory (SAIC Rep. No. 84-04-178). McLean, VA: Science Applications International.

Tennyson, R. D., & Buttrey, T. (1980). Advisement and management strategies as design variables in computer-assisted instruction. *Educational Communication and Technology Journal, 28,* 169–176. Reprinted in D. F. Walker and R. D. Hess (Eds.), *Instructional software: Principles and perspectives for design and use.* Belmont, CA: Wadsworth, 1984.

Tiemann, P. W., & Markle, S. M. (1983). *Analyzing instructional content: A guide to instruction and evaluation* (2nd ed.). Champaign, IL: Stipes.

TRADOC. (1975). *Interservice procedures for instructional systems development: Executive summary and model.* U.S. Army TRADOC Pamphlet 350-30.

Weiss, D. J. (1979). Computerized adaptive achievement testing. In H. O'Neil, Jr. (Ed.), *Procedures for instructional systems development.* New York: Academic Press.

Weiss, K. M. (1978). A comparison of forward and backward procedures for the acquisition of response chains in humans. *Journal of the Experimental Analysis of Behavior, 29,* 255–259.

White, M. A. (1983). Toward a psychology of electronic learning. In M. A. White (Ed.), *The future of electronic learning.* New York: Academic Press.

White, O.R., & Haring, N.G. (1976). *Exceptional teaching.* Columbus, OH: Charles E. Merrill.

Wightman, D. C., & Sistrunk, F. (1987). Part-task training strategies in simulated carrier landing final-approach training. *Human Factors, 29,* 245–254.

Williges, B. H., & Williges, R. C. (1984). Dialog design considerations for interactive computer systems. *Human Factors Review, 1984,* 167–206.

Woolf, B., & Cunningham, P. A. (1987, Summer). Multiple knowledge sources in intelligent teaching systems. *IEEE Expert, 2*(2), 41–54.

Woolf, B., & McDonald, D. D. (1984, September). Building a computer tutor: Design issues. *Computer,* pp. 61–73.

Zinn, K. L. (1981). Computer-based instruction in Europe and Japan. In H. F. O'Neil, Jr. (Ed.), *Computer-based instruction: A state-of-the-art assessment.* New York: Academic Press.

Index